Lenin

Founder of the Soviet Union

by Abraham Resnick

 CHILDRENS PRESS®
CHICAGO

DEDICATION
To Gilda

PICTURE ACKNOWLEDGMENTS

Novosti Press Agency—Frontispiece, pages 5, 8 (2 photos), 26,
57 (3 photos), 58 (2 photos), 59 (2 photos), 60 (2 photos), 61 (2 photos),
62 2 photos), 63 (2 photos), 64, 76, 84, 104, 110 (2 photos), 118
Cover illustration by Len W. Meents

Library of Congress Cataloging in Publication Data

Resnick, Abraham.
  Lenin: founder of the Soviet Union.

  Includes index.
  Summary: A biography of the leader of the 1917 Bolshevik
Revolution who formulated the official Communist ideology
and became the first head of the Soviet state.
  1. Lenin, Vladimir Il'ich, 1870-1924—Juvenile literature.
2. Heads of states—Soviet Union—Biography—Juvenile
literature. 3. Revolutionists—Soviet Union—Biography—
Juvenile literature. 4. Soviet Union—History—Revolution,
1917-1921—Juvenile literature.
[1. Lenin, Vladimir Il'ich, 1870-1924. 2. Heads of state.
3. Revolutionists. 4. Soviet Union—History—Revolution,
1917-1921] I. Title.
DK254.L455R47   1987   947.084'1'0924 [B][92]   87-13249
ISBN 0-516-03260-7

1 2 3 4 5 6 7 8 9 10 R 96 95 94 93 92 91 90 89 88 87

Table of Contents

Above: A statue at Gorki depicting the death of Lenin.

Below: A monument to Lenin in Lenin Square in Ulyanovsk

Chapter 1

LENIN—BIGGER THAN LIFE

In the Soviet Union today, hardly a moment passes without some kind of tribute to, or acknowledgment of, Lenin. Though he died in 1924, Lenin is still the greatest hero of the Soviet people. Each day of the year, in all kinds of weather, thousands of citizens line up in Moscow's Red Square, waiting hours to enter the Lenin Mausoleum. Inside there is a closely guarded, dark marble chamber in which an embalmed and mummylike Lenin lies in a glass tomb. For most of the countless visitors, the visit to the burial crypt is a proud pilgrimage to the country's national shrine. It allows them an opportunity to pay their solemn respect to a man held in greater esteem than anyone else in Soviet history.

Lenin is remembered fondly in the USSR. Reminders of the man and his contribution to Soviet society take on many different forms. They are visible everywhere. His boyhood home in Ulyanovsk, a city that took his family name, is a very popular tourist attraction. Petrograd, renamed Leningrad, is Russia's second-largest city. Throughout the USSR it is very common for streets, buildings, enterprises, and farms to have the name of Lenin. Museums, stadiums, theaters, Pioneer camps, schools, and libraries bear the name Lenin as well. There is even a Soviet icebreaker called *Lenin*.

Sometimes pictures or busts of Lenin are displayed in Soviet homes. Practically every public building provides a picture of Lenin in its entry hall. Hundreds of books and articles about Lenin are published each year and are widely read by young and old alike.

Numerous plays and motion pictures have been made about his life. And Lenin's teaching can be found at all levels of the school curriculum. Hardly a city square or park is without a commanding statue of Lenin. It is not unusual to see floral wreaths and bridal bouquets being placed at the base of Lenin monuments. Newlyweds follow a tradition of visiting the local Lenin memorial or monument after the wedding ceremony. His likeness appears on billboards and giant red banners all over the land. His greatness is constantly being emphasized with slogans calling upon every man, woman, and child to do their utmost to live up to his teachings.

Lenin was a man who made history by turning Russia upside down. He began a revolution that was heard round the world—and its reverberations are still being heard.

Chapter 2

GROWING UP IN TSARIST RUSSIA

In the year 988 a ruling prince named Vladimir I, later known as St. Vladimir, the first Christian grand duke of Kiev, became a Christian and converted Russia to Christianity. Centuries later, on April 22, 1870, an infant was baptized with the same historic name in a church in Simbirsk, a small city located on the Volga River, about 425 miles east of Moscow. (Today the city is named Ulyanovsk after him.) Born Vladimir Ilyich Ulyanov, he grew up in Russia at a time when tsars, princes, noblemen, and village priests handed down the laws that determined how people were to live. But upon reaching manhood, Vladimir Ulyanov was to become a famous revolutionary leader known as Lenin and he, more than anyone else, helped to bring drastic changes to the land.

The Ulyanovs were a closely knit family. The father, Ilya, and the mother, Maria, showed great devotion to each other and to their children. Vladimir was the third child in a family of six. When he was born, his sister Anna was six years old and and his brother Alexander was four. Vladimir was followed by Olga, Dimitri, and Maria.

Their father had a university education, which he had earned on a scholarship. His record in school was so outstanding that he was selected to study under one of the most respected mathematicians in all of Russia, Professor N.L. Lobachevsky, one of the discoverers of non-Euclidean geometry. Upon graduation from the university, Ilya Ulyanov obtained a position as a teacher of physics and mathematics, and in due time became an inspector of schools for the tsar's government in the Simbirsk province. This position gave him the title, "Excellency," the same rank as a general in the military.

Their mother came from a large, cultured, middle-class but privileged family. Good books and musical instruments were important parts of her household environment. There were servants in Maria's childhood home and she was able to find time to garden, read, and learn to speak German, French, and English. Her father had been a physician. In his forties he retired to a small country estate in the province of Kazan.

Vladimir spent many happy summer weeks during his childhood and youth at Kokushkino, the village where his mother's family estate was located. He especially enjoyed traveling there with his family, taking a long steamboat ride on the Volga River from his home in Simbirsk. Once there, Vladimir enjoyed playing with his brothers, sisters, and cousins. He learned how to swim and row a boat with ease. He went fishing, rode horses, hiked, played chess and billiards, and did his share of picking forest berries and mushrooms. On rainy days there were always children's books to read, pictures to draw, and word puzzles and games to make up. Vladimir was a very imaginative, energetic, and active youngster. He seemed to excel in everything he undertook.

As a lad, though somewhat undersized, Vladimir seemed larger than his actual height. His frame was powerfully stocky, if not bulky, and he was often teased about his appearance. The family sometimes called him "Kubyshka," which means "little strong box" in Russian. But most of all he was called "Volodya," the Russian nickname for Vladimir.

Volodya had a marked resemblance to his father. This became more obvious when, in his twenties, he began to lose his hair. Another of Volodya's distinctive physical characteristics was his facial features. His wide-set almond-shaped eyes, high cheekbones, small ears, flattened nose, and full lips gave him a kind of Asiatic look, not too uncommon for many eastern Russians.

Photographs taken of the young Volodya show that he was neat and tidy in appearance. Later in life he grew a small pointed beard and prominent mustache, which were always kept trimmed. His dark blond hair was never long in the back or unruly, which was the style of freethinkers, terrorists, and revolutionaries of that time.

The boyhood years Volodya spent in Simbirsk were very happy. Describing that time, he spoke of "living in easy circumstances." Telling about his childhood he said, "We did not know hunger or cold; we were surrounded by all sorts of cultural opportunities and stimuli, books, music, and diversions." There was a nice family atmosphere of good feeling and affection for each other.

As often as possible, their mother told the children stories and read aloud to them. They all enjoyed the family sing-alongs she led, and her piano playing was admired. She not only taught all her children how to play the piano, but how to read and write. Volodya learned how to read at age five. The Ulyanovs even produced a weekly handwritten newspaper for themselves to which each of the family members contributed original news items, prose, and poetry.

Although the family newspaper was called *Subbotnick*, which means the Sabbath, in the Ulyanov home it was hardly directed toward religion. The father was quite religious, having been raised in the Russian Orthodox faith. But the mother, a Lutheran in her childhood, rarely attended church. Nevertheless, perhaps out of respect for the father, certain religious customs and Russian Orthodox holiday traditions were upheld for Christmas, Easter, and the Lenten fast. Still, their father did not insist that the children observe any particular religion. As they reached their teens, the children began to turn away from formal religious rites. Volodya stopped believing in God when he was sixteen.

When Volodya was eight years old, the Ulyanovs moved to a fairly large and comfortable two-story, wood frame house on a quiet, tree-lined street. The well-tended home was enclosed by a wooded fence and in the family orchard behind the house each of the children had a garden section and fruit trees to care for. A coach house and croquet court were also out back.

The house had many windows, each covered with white curtains, and the rooms were very attractive and bright. The dining room was the most spacious room in the house. In a number of the rooms, there were study desks and books filled many of the shelves. The display of writing sets, chess boards, piano, period furnishings, sterling silver, and brass samovar readily gave the impression that this was the home of a respectable middle-class family.

Volodya's room at the top of the stairs was simply furnished. There was a plain white metal bed, yellow wallpaper, a candle and candlestick, a hanging wall case for books, a desk and chair, and a map of the world—the same world that would someday be shaken by the great events attributed to the man who was just a young boy when he slept in that room.

Though Volodya was usually nice to his brothers and sisters, there were times when his conduct was a bit disturbing. On occasion he could be temperamental, abrupt, and self-centered. These characteristics became more noticeable during his later adolescent years.

When he was a small child his father would discipline Volodya by making him sit in the "black chair" of his study until he was ready to behave himself properly. But many times the punishment was short-lived, for Volodya would quickly fall asleep in the chair.

If the domestic order and discipline demanded by his father failed at times to reach Volodya, his behavior at school was just about perfect. When it came to applying himself diligently to studies, young Volodya turned out to be as serious and dedicated as his father had been in school. Early on, it was obvious that Volodya was exceptionally gifted and talented. He admired his father's intelligence and willingness to put his heart and soul into his job as an education official and teacher of teachers.

In the province of Simbirsk, Ilya Ulyanov stood out from all other educators for his tireless efforts and exceptional performance of his duties. Often working long hours, at times seven days a week to promote and construct local schools, his devotion to the importance of education was readily absorbed by his son.

At age nine Vladimir entered the first class at the classical *gymnasium*. He immediately became the top student in his class. Furthermore, his conduct was so good that he was frequently singled out as a model for other students.

Study and learning came easily to Vladimir. He especially liked Latin, Greek, Russian literature, history, and geography. He was particularly fond of reading the classics, the writings of ancient authors. In class he paid very close attention to his teachers' explanations. Once at home he immediately turned to preparing his assignments. Afterward his father, when not away in the outlying villages, would quiz him on his daily lessons and understanding of the course.

Vladimir's grades were, with the exception of logic, the highest possible marks a student could earn. After a number of years his record was so exceptional that his father became worried. He feared Vladimir might become bored with schooling and develop poor work habits. But this never happened. His parents, never ones to brag about him or permit him to be praised before others, were secretly very happy with his success.

Equally delighted with Vladimir's school record was the headmaster of the high school. This is what he wrote in the letter of recommendation given to Vladimir Ulyanov:

> Quite talented, invariably diligent, prompt and reliable, Ulyanov was first in all his classes, and upon graduation was awarded a gold medal as the most meritorious pupil in achieve-

ment, growth, and conduct. There is not a single instance on record, either in school or outside of it, of Ulyanov's evoking by word or deed any adverse opinion from the authorities and teachers of this school.

But one line in the headmaster's report was glaringly different from the rest:

> Upon closer examination of Ulyanov's home life and character, I could not but observe in him an excessive introversion and lack of sociability even with acquaintances, and outside the school even with fellow students who were the school's pride and joy, in short, an aversion to companionship.

The headmaster signed his name, Fyodor Kerensky. Many years later his son, Alexander Kerensky, would become premier of the first provisional government of Russia after the revolution in 1917—and be overthrown by none other than the most outstanding graduate of Simbirsk High School, Vladimir Ilyich Ulyanov, by then known as Lenin.

Chapter 3

THE EXECUTION OF A BROTHER

In 1886, when Vladimir was nearly sixteen, the happy Ulyanov family was struck by tragedy. Vladimir's father died very unexpectedly of a cerebral hemorrhage on January 12. His older brother, Alexander, was in St. Petersburg at the time studying at the university. Since Vladimir was the next oldest son, he immediately took on many of the responsibilities normally performed by the man of the house.

Vladimir showed much concern about his mother and tried to help her in every way. Despite his own great sorrow, he kept busy and concentrated on his studies.

In 1887, when Vladimir was in his last year at school, a second tragedy befell the Ulyanovs. Alexander was arrested in St. Petersburg for his part in an attempt to assassinate Tsar Alexander III. Vladimir was the first to learn of the arrest and it was he who had to inform his mother of the shocking news.

Alexander's personality and interests were different from

Vladimir's. Alexander tended to be much more involved in nature study, science, and carpentry than his younger brother. He also was more tactful, mild mannered, and even-tempered. Vladimir looked up to Alexander as a model, often read the same books, and liked to follow his example.

Alexander, it seems, was a very private person, and rather idealistic. His ways were so secretive, however, that no one in the family had ever suspected that he would become a participant in a conspiracy to kill Tsar Alexander III. But, as the facts of the plot became known and the circumstances revealed, it was obvious that Alexander Ulyanov was guilty of the charges brought against him and his fellow terrorists by the authorities.

In 1887, the Russian people had not been granted the economic opportunities and political freedoms allowed in many of the more progressive countries. There was no freedom of assembly, no free speech. Russia remained backward and life there was hard for the serfs, common people, and members of the lower classes.

In this feudal system, landlords had large estates. The serfs, or peasant farmers who lived on the land, had to pay high rents and provide long hours of service. A serf's holdings usually included a small long house or hut, a narrow strip of land, and a few animals. The serf got very little from his field patch. The landlord took most of the peasant's crop as rent payment and as part of his taxes. The serf knew that if he did not pay these taxes, he would be severely punished.

Wealth, privileges, land ownership, and luxurious lifestyles were enjoyed by aristocrats and nobles. Churchmen, military officers, high-ranking government officials (such as Vladimir's father), rich merchants, and mill owners also were well off.

The Russian Orthodox church was a very important part of the people's lives. The serfs followed the religion faithfully and believed the clergy to be above reproach. The fact that the priests wore robes often embroidered in gold and silver and miters glittering with jewels did not disturb the serfs.

Year after year there were hopes that life would improve for the lowly serfs and workers. But progress was very slow. Factory pay was meager for long hard hours of work, and obtaining an education was almost impossible for the lower classes. Periods of starvation in Russia were commonplace; housing conditions were wretched; and for those who dared to demonstrate or strike against the existing conditions, police reprisals were often brutal. Punishment might mean long-term imprisonment, even exile to Siberia.

At the top of this autocratic and unjust society was the tsar, Alexander III, always protected by his palace guards, cossack forces (the tsar's cavalry unit), and secret police. His word was law. He was the absolute emperor of all of Russia. The people revered him and called him "Our Own Dear Father." They *expected* him to live in luxury. The tsar surrounded himself with the greatest of comforts and pleasures—the finest clothes, imported tapestries, rare jewels, luscious foods, servants, entertainers, and the latest means of transportation.

A staff of hundreds was at the tsar's call, ready to provide him with any luxury, or cater to any fancy he might desire. Yet, more often than not, the tsar was remote and isolated from the people. It seemed that he knew little of their real plight, and cared even less.

The previous tsar, Alexander II, had been a more liberal and benevolent tsar than Alexander III. He had tried to free the serfs and bring about political changes, but he was assassinated by revolutionaries in March 1881. This brought his son, Alexander III, to the throne. He was an autocrat, a ruler with unlimited power, who used strong measures to halt any progress by the people and so became a target for murder as well.

Alexander, Vladimir, their fellow students, and many other Russians, including the middle class and some well-to-do people, had become aware of these great differences. They became increasingly disturbed about the inequities. They had read or heard reports telling about the life of grandeur led by the tsar and the magnificence of his palaces with their fantastic art, sculpture, waterfalls, chandeliers, and highly polished parquet floors.

They saw firsthand how the peasants lived in crowded

contaminated wooden barracks that had no heat, running water, or inside bathroom facilities. They saw people thrown in jail because they could not pay their taxes. The Ulyanov brothers observed that the children of peasants and workers did not go to school and as a result were unable to read or write. They saw small children being forced to work under harsh conditions in the fields and factories. They were quite disturbed by these injustices.

Though Alexander Ulyanov was part of a secret organization that planned the assassination of Tsar Alexander III, he was not the ringleader. Revolutionary ideas were being embraced by many groups. There were a number of secret organizations. Some only wanted reforms. But others, the extremists, preferred no government or organized society at all.

The would-be terrorists had no money, organization, or training. Alexander even had to sell a gold medal he had received as a scholastic award to raise money to make a bomb and obtain pistols and ammunition. Alexander had a good background in science and he was willing to read about explosives in the library. So he was assigned the task of manufacturing the dynamite device.

Alexander and his student cohorts did not realize that just prior to the assassination attempt, some of the group were already under the scrutiny of police detectives. It seems that Tsar Alexander was scheduled to make a ceremonial inspection of St. Petersburg, the capital, on March 13, and was to proceed along Nevsky Prospect, the city's broadest boulevard, in his most elegant horse-drawn carriage.

It was on that day that three of Alexander's companions were arrested on the boulevard while waiting for the tsar's procession. One carried a large hollow book with a bomb in it. Another had a pistol. He attempted to shoot at the policeman confronting him, but the weapon failed to fire. The third student, once in custody at the police station, suddenly whipped out a cardboard box that he had hidden in his coat pocket and threw it to the floor. The enclosed bomb also failed to go off. Obviously the would-be assassins were amateurs. They were better with ideas than with weapons.

After the three students were arrested for their part in the plot, it did not take long before Alexander Ulyanov also was taken by the police. His mother immediately set out for St. Petersburg. While visiting him in jail she found him to be the same calm lad he had always been. He was not ready to show any regret or sorrow, even if that could have helped save his life. Instead, he was ready to accept all the blame himself.

During the trial Alexander spoke out against the existing social order, proclaimed that a revolution would come about, and justified using terror to force drastic changes in the Russian form of government. At the end, in a matter-of-fact and frank manner, he told his judges: "There is no finer death than death for one's country's sake; such a death holds no terror for sincere and honest men. I had but one aim: to help the unfortunate Russian people." Alexander Ulyanov and his young comrades were sentenced to death by hanging.

Alexander's mother stayed in St. Petersburg until the day of the execution. When she returned to Simbirsk in a state of quiet despair, she found the younger children under Vladimir's care crying and very emotionally upset. Vladimir seemed to take on his brother's calm disposition and tried to ease the situation as best he could. He refused to show his inner feelings of pain and suffering. He became more reserved.

Once again he plunged into his studies and, with only a few weeks remaining before graduation, began to work in preparation for the university entrance examination.

Vladimir could not forget Alexander. Could he, or should he, avenge his brother's death? He often wondered if his brother had chosen the right path of struggle and would say: "That is not the path we shall take. It is not the right one." Already he began to realize that it was not the tsars who needed to be replaced—but the entire "rotten system that needed to go."

Vladimir Ulyanov as a student in Samara, 1891

Chapter 4

EXILE TO SIBERIA

Not long after Vladimir completed high school, he applied to the school of law at Kazan University. Because of his brother Alexander's activities, it was not certain that he would be able to enroll in any university. Those who thought they knew him best, like Principal Kerensky and many of the teachers, advised the young graduate that he was better suited for the school of literature and letters than law. But Vladimir remained stubborn about his choice. Kerensky wrote a strong letter of recommendation to the rector of the faculty of law at Kazan and Vladimir was approved for admission.

Vladimir entered the university in August 1887. Shortly thereafter his mother, anxious to get away from the local stigma associated with her son's hanging, decided to move the remaining family to Kazan. She rented an apartment close to the university, allowing Vladimir to live at home and walk to classes.

At this time the revolutionary feeling in Russia was continuing to spread. Students throughout the land were demonstrating against the state of affairs in the country. The government in turn, along with university authorities, began to clamp down on student protesters and became quite strict with student organizations that were being formed in opposition to government policies. Student inspectors were placed on the campuses for the purpose of spying on those who were bent on violating the rules.

One evening a large portion of the student body at Kazan University staged a protest meeting in support of a student in Moscow, who was given a very harsh punishment for striking a student inspector. They also demanded changes in the government's restrictions on students' rights. The crowd became loud. When a student inspector appeared to order the assembly to halt the meeting, he was immediately attacked, triggering a nasty melee.

More than one hundred students were arrested that night. Among those placed in custody was Vladimir Ulyanov, despite the fact that he had been a silent observer and had not participated in the riot. Apparently he had been watched by the police who, with their knowledge of the fate of his brother, found Vladimir an easy person to blame for the disorder.

Vladimir was expelled from the university, along with forty-five others, and he also was forced to leave the city of

Kazan. The government authorities made him a scapegoat as an example to his fellow students.

At this time Vladimir was against revolution, hoping changes would come by peaceful and legal means. He was thinking like a lawyer then. Yet, gradually, he was becoming more and more concerned about the ever-present injustices in his country.

It has been reported that a police guard escorting Vladimir out of the city asked, "Why do you revolt, young man? You are up against a stone wall . . ." Vladimir was said to have answered: "A wall, yes, but a crumbling one . . . which will soon collapse."

The family went to live in Kokushkino where Vladimir decided to pursue his studies on his own. With little to distract him at the old family homestead, he began to devour book after book. But he was not only preoccupied with law books. He began to read the writings of Karl Marx, and became fascinated by the theories of this early revolutionary.

Though Karl Marx was known mostly to Socialists and revolutionaries during his lifetime, many people all over the world now read his doctrines about economics, philosophy, and politics.

Marx was born in the German Rhineland in 1818, the son of a successful lawyer and grandson of a rabbi, a Jewish clergyman. He, too, studied law and philosophy, but his radical ideas published in a paper he edited in Cologne led to the censorship of his views. Facing arrest, he fled to Paris in 1844, but was expelled in 1849. For the remaining thirty-four years of his life he made his home in London.

Marx was fortunate to find Frederick Engels, who shared his ideas, helped sponsor him, and took care of his living expenses. Marx and Engels wrote a booklet, published in 1848, entitled *Communist Manifesto*, which simply explained the principal beliefs of communism. The three volumes of Marx's chief work, *Das Kapital*, which declared that all history is determined by economics, were published over the period of 1867-94 (the last two volumes were edited by Engels after Marx's death).

Marx wanted all industries to be controlled by the state and not by individuals. He felt it was socially unfair for an individual, or individuals, to profit, while the workers did not. He believed that a class struggle existed between the exploiters (the "bourgeoisie") and the oppressed working people (the "proletariat"). He went on to predict that the capitalists, or exploiters, would be overthrown, a classless society would then come about, and there would no longer be a need for revolutions. It was envisioned that everyone would be guided by the rule, "From each according to his ability; to each according to his needs."

Eventually there would be no need for a state. It would "wither away," he contended. But, in order to hurry the process along, revolution might be required. That is why Marx took part in revolutionary movements in Germany, and sometimes called upon others to rise in violent opposition to the existing order of things.

By the end of the 1880s, young intellectuals in Russia were interested in Marx's ideas. The more Vladimir read works by writers espousing the need for change in society, the greater became his awareness that he needed to become involved. And when his request to be readmitted to the university was denied, he began to show frustration and bitterness. He became extremely arrogant, sarcastic, and temperamental. With almost no prospect of a professional career ahead and time on his hands, Vladimir's thoughts turned to the possibility and merit of eventual revolution.

His mother, very much concerned about her son, thought it might be good for Vladimir to become a kind of gentleman farmer. She received a governmental widow's pension, which helped support the family. She sold the house in Simbirsk and purchased a small wooded estate in Samara (now Kuybyshev) on the Volga River for summer farming. Though the family held the property for four years, it did not take that long to see that Vladimir was not cut out to be a farm manager.

Vladimir's mother persisted for three years in trying to obtain permission from the authorities at St. Petersburg University to allow him to take the law examination without having to attend classes. When they finally agreed—probably thinking that it would in all likelihood be an impossible task anyway—it took Vladimir a mere eighteen months of diligent studying at home to prepare for the test. For all others it required at least four years of university work before they were ready to sit for the examination.

Vladimir proved to be an exception. In 1891 he passed the two-part, eighteen-section examination with a perfect score, and, at the age of twenty-one, received a diploma of the first degree with permission to practice law in Russia.

The perfect score that Vladimir received in the law exam is miraculous in itself. Just before taking the spring section of the test in St. Petersburg, his younger sister Olga, studying at a teachers' institute in that city, became seriously ill with typhoid fever. It was Vladimir who rushed her to the hospital, where she died on May 20, the fourth anniversary of his brother's execution.

As a young lawyer in Samara, Vladimir mostly defended the poor or those who were victimized by the state of affairs. His most satisfying case, however, was one in which he defended himself.

A wealthy merchant owned a service that ferried people across the Volga River. The merchant paid a fee to the government for the right to operate this service. One day Vladimir was in a hurry and did not want to wait for the ferry, so he hired a boatman to row him across. The owner warned Vladimir that he could not hire his own rowboat.

Vladimir felt that his lawful right to move about freely was being challenged, and he ordered the boatman he had hired to row him immediately to the east bank of the river. The ferry owner quickly set out to intercept the rowboat and forced it to return to the west bank.

Extremely upset by this maneuver, Vladimir took the ferry service owner to court, on the grounds that he had interfered with Vladimir's basic rights. Sure enough, after a year's delay, Vladimir won the case, his principle was upheld, and the ferry owner was sentenced to jail for one month. But, all in all, he failed to enjoy the practice of law and even found it rather uninteresting.

While living in Samara, Vladimir frequently attended secret meetings held by expelled university students and revolutionaries. At these sessions he learned about the philosophies of revolutionaries, how they recruited new members, how they were organized, their secret codes and passwords, their fake passports, and how to send invisible ink messages.

In 1893 Vladimir was restless and tired of small-town law work, and he decided to move to St. Petersburg where many small cells of reformers and revolutionaries were being formed. These cells usually limited their membership to six people in order to meet secretly in apartments away from the surveillance of the police. St. Petersburg also had a rapidly growing number of factories where the workers had to labor under very severe, if not inhuman, conditions.

Vladimir was ready to take action by spreading Marxist ideas of revolution directly to the industrial workers (not the peasantry) by teaching them how to sabotage and to organize strikes, and by teaching them how to become revolutionaries themselves. By now Vladimir had become a full-time revolutionary with the desire to overthrow the government.

Shortly after his arrival in St. Petersburg, Vladimir met Nadezhda "Nadya" Krupskaya at a small social gathering. She was involved in teaching illiterate workers how to read and write. Though she was almost two years older than Vladimir and not overly attractive, he enjoyed her companionship.

Krupskaya was quite tall and thin, had a broad forehead, straight, sharply cut, center-parted short hair, big blue eyes, puckered lips, and a snub nose. There was something very special about her. Her manner was feminine, compassionate, and dignified. Especially appealing to Vladimir were her intelligence and her genuine dedication to the cause.

Vladimir, on the other hand, though only twenty-four years old at this time, had become quite bald, with noticeable lines on his face. In fact, some of his friends often referred to him as the "old man," but this nickname was really in respect for his wisdom and knowledge. Krupskaya was charmed by his great intelligence, forceful manner of speech, and strong convictions.

Though they did not agree on all revolutionary matters,

they respected one another and enjoyed their long talks and walks along the city's canals and riverbanks. They began to build a very close personal relationship, and were exceptionally supportive of one another.

Vladimir had little respect for lawyers. He regarded them as "professional windbags." Nevertheless, he practiced some law in St. Petersburg, working as an assistant to a liberal lawyer named M.F. Volkenstein. He spent much of his time in direct action as an undercover operator—not at the direction of his employer, although Volkenstein probably knew what he was doing. Disguised as a workman, he would visit factories, try to stir up interest in revolution among the workers, and leave them with secretly published pamphlets, illegal newspapers, and books.

Some of the books were provided by a well-to-do woman named Alexandra Kalmykova, who sympathized with the goals of the revolutionaries. Mrs. Kalmykova had a bookstore and a publishing house. Bent on improving the lot of the exploited factory workers, Mrs. Kalmykova published some of the underground materials herself. Then she would make them available for sale very cheaply at her own bookshop.

Vladimir was barely able to support himself at this time. His loyal mother, who had conflicting feelings about his activities, managed to send him money. Other funds came from Mrs. Kalmykova.

Learning about Marxism suddenly became a popular fad in Russia with "progressive" thinkers. Even the government censors, not fully aware of the ramifications of Marxist theories, and more concerned with bomb throwers, allowed certain writings to pass their reviews. They used the permissive term "legal Marxism."

Vladimir took advantage of the new climate of the period by launching his own writing career with a series of three notebooks in defense of Marxism, entitled *Little Yellow Books*. Writing under the pen name of K. Tulin, Vladimir wrote an essay critical of the conventional views of Marxism held by certain influential authors. But his critique was seized by the police as being too rebellious against lawful authority.

Little by little Vladimir was becoming well known as a highly respected authority on how to put the theories of Marxism into practice. Of course this type of expertise was hardly appreciated in governmental circles, and Vladimir now, more than ever, came under the watchful eyes of the Okhrana, the tsarist secret police.

Avoiding the police, running to factories, attending secret cell meetings, and writing political tracts put a lot of stress on Vladimir, and his overwork brought on severe stomach upsets, followed by pneumonia. His mother and his sister Anna came from Moscow, where they were living, to try to nurse him back to health.

Becoming convinced that he needed a "change of scenery," he used his illness as an excuse to travel abroad. Though he had been turned down twice before, this time he managed to obtain a passport. It was not unusual for revolutionaries, who wanted to change the Russian system, to carry out their work in another country. So Vladimir set out for Switzerland in the spring of 1895 and stayed at a Swiss health resort. Then he went on to meet and confer with famous revolutionaries in Geneva, Zurich, Paris, and Berlin. His mother continued to send him money for his basic needs.

Georgi Plekhanov, a well-known writer of social revolutionary themes, and Paul B. Axelrod, another highly regarded revolutionary, who had been forced to leave Russia in 1880, were anxious to meet the young Marxist. Plekhanov, as it turned out, was more moderate and more willing to work with the slower-paced liberals in their move toward Marxism. Axelrod seemed more sympathetic to Vladimir's objectives, but he too was concerned that the base of power must include all the left-wing groups working together in their revolutionary struggle.

Vladimir argued for a faster time schedule. He advocated violence as the way to overthrow the existing order. Plekhanov was much less optimistic that the Russian worker was ready for revolution.

Increasingly Vladimir was becoming more impatient with the lack of movement toward the overthrow of the government. Forceful measures, he now began to realize, would have to be taken soon. After all, hadn't Marx also advocated the use of violence if need be? Vladimir maintained, stubbornly, that any means, including terror, might be justified if it served the sacred cause of revolution.

What, on the other hand, Vladimir failed to take into account was that Marx argued that it was fraudulent to incite the people without first producing a firm basis for revolutionary action.

In Paris, which Vladimir enjoyed immensely, he was able to improve his French. He became acquainted with the daughter and son-in-law of Karl Marx, which excited him since, in a way, Marx had been Vladimir's mentor. It soon became apparent to the important men who engaged Vladimir in debate and discussion that he would be a very effective leader to take charge of the movement in Russia.

During his four months abroad visiting libraries and making revolutionary contacts, Vladimir's activities were well known to the Russian police. When he returned home they inspected all the articles in his trunk, but were totally fooled when they failed to uncover the trunk's false bottom. In it were forbidden papers that if discovered could have meant immediate imprisonment for Vladimir.

In addition to the illegal revolutionary political tracts and pamphlets, Vladimir was bold enough to smuggle across the border a hectograph, which was strictly prohibited. This was a duplicating device, using a gelatin pad to print from original writing or typed matter.

It did not take Vladimir long to resume his revolutionary tactics after he returned to St. Petersburg. But now, using various aliases, he became more of an agitator than a propagandist. Julius Martov, a young intellectual and new-found friend of whom Vladimir was very fond, convinced him that he needed to incite the workers to strike, to try to win political freedom along with economic gains for them, and to concentrate more on the overthrow of the tsarist autocracy itself.

Vladimir then moved toward uniting the many Marxist groups under the banner of "Union of Struggle for the Emancipation of the Working Class." But, a short time after its formation in December 1895, forty members, Vladimir included, were arrested when a trusted member turned out to be a police informer planted within their ranks.

For the next fourteen months Vladimir was imprisoned in St. Petersburg with other political inmates. Because he was accustomed to a frugal, self-disciplined life-style, he was able to cope with prison life without becoming overly depressed. He read, studied, and exercised in his cell, doing fifty sit-ups a day. He figured out a way to play chess with men in nearby cells by signaling moves tapped out on cell-block walls. Luckily, the prison had a good library and with the forbidden books that his mother and sister brought him on their regular visits, time passed rather quickly. Even his health improved.

While serving his prison term, Vladimir perfected an ingenious technique for carrying out secret correspondence with revolutionaries on the outside. Milk or lemon juice, ordinarily invisible, were dabbed in the form of tiny dots and dashes onto printed letters of the pages of books and printed articles being brought in and out of prison. It was found that when the milk- or juice-formed codes plotted on the pages were dipped in strong tea or heated and held to a light, they could be read and decoded. Vladimir became highly skilled at making "inkwells" out of hidden fluid-laden pieces of bread. When the guards would become suspicious, or when surprise inspections of the cells were made, Vladimir would quickly swallow the evidence. Once, in secret correspondence, he jokingly wrote a friend: "Today I have eaten six inkwells."

From prison, Vladimir was able to stay in touch with revolutionary activities. He cleverly laid the plans for some strikes and factory walkouts. But his prison stay was to end in February 1897, when he was informed that he was to be exiled to Siberia, under police watch, for a sentence of three years.

Chapter 5

THE EMERGENCE OF LENIN

Fortunately for Vladimir the exile in Siberia turned out to be much less harsh than it was for many other prisoners. Since he was the son of a former government official, his sentence was relatively lenient.

He was banished to the small village of Shushenskoye, more than two thousand miles from Moscow, in eastern Siberia, not far from the Yenisei River. The climate was a lot more temperate than the bitter conditions of the northern tundra, with its frozen swamplands, long dark frigid winters, and mosquito filled short summer months. Besides, Shushenskoye only had two political prisoners, and Vladimir was allowed to rent a simply furnished room in a wooden cottage.

Though his life in Shushenskoye was quite lonely, the peaceful atmosphere there enabled Vladimir to continue with his writing and correspondence. His family once again remained supportive and never failed to send him money and books. The townspeople liked him very much and even asked him for legal advice on occasion, which he freely gave. Vladimir enjoyed the food from the nearby farms. He easily gained weight during his stay, despite the fact that he was actively enjoying swimming, walking, fishing, hunting, ice skating, and sleigh riding.

In many respects, strange as it may seem, Vladimir's years in exile may have been the happiest of his life. He made great progress on his writing and translations. He was able to write thirty different position papers. His health was good. He met often with other political exiles in the region. And in the spring of 1898, Nadezhda Krupskaya, accompanied by her mother, was able to join him.

Eight months after Vladimir's arrest, Krupskaya was sentenced to a three-year stay in Siberia also. She was given permission to serve her sentence in Shushenskoye on the condition that she and Vladimir marry. Their marriage took place there in a church ceremony, as required by law, despite the fact that they were both atheists.

During his term of exile Vladimir was hardly ever idle. He read philosophy and great Russian classic literature. He especially craved reading views of Marxism by others. Vladimir also studied and improved his English and German. Krupskaya helped him translate into Russian *The Theory and Practice of Trade Unionism*, written by two famous British Socialists. In addition, writing under the pen name of V. Ilyin (during his lifetime he assumed many different pseudonyms), he completed his major socioeconomic study, *The Development of Capitalism in Russia*. This book became Vladimir's most important contribution to Russian economic thought, and helped establish him as a specialist in Marxist economics throughout Europe.

As Vladimir kept up his coded correspondence with many of his revolution-bent friends, and as he was able to read the underground pamphlets and tracts smuggled into Shushenskoye, he became deeply concerned that much of the great enthusiasm for a revolution was beginning to lessen. Some of his comrades, he thought, seemed prone to compromise.

Police persecution became more pronounced and more and more men and women in the movement were being sent away. Only a handful of people attended the first "congress" of Socialists held in Minsk in 1898. One proved to be a spy within their ranks and shortly thereafter eight of the group of Russian Marxists were arrested and sent into exile. Nevertheless, the participants had founded a new political party—the Russian Social Democratic party.

The new party supported Vladimir's brand of Marxism, which advocated the establishment of socialism by appealing to the factory workers to overthrow the tsar. The workers, it was thought, were more susceptible to their ideas, more intellectually advanced than the peasants, and concentrated in Russia's political centers. "The proletariat alone," Vladimir wrote, "can be front-line-fighters for political liberty and democratic institutions." The rival group, the Social Revolutionaries, wanted Marxism to be established by first inciting Russian serfs to rise up against the system.

Vladimir's contention to first focus on the workers ranks was at least in part due to his perspective that it would be very difficult to confiscate all the land from the peasants, who at this time in Russia outnumbered workers eight to one. A number of the peasants, he felt, were small-scale capitalists, while others seemed reasonably satisfied with their lives on "their" soil, living in the *mirs*, which were communities of peasant farmers. Besides, because of the nature of farming and the need to share in the purchase of equipment and fertilizer and assist each other at planting and harvests, the cooperative movement had already taken hold. Yet, the peasants were weak and disorganized politically. Once Vladimir even referred to the peasants as "bourgeoisie in disguise."

Other groups espousing less drastic proposals for bringing about change were being formed, and Vladimir became more anxious than ever to get back into the thick of the action and fight for his approach. The Russian Social Democrats were more interested in mapping out a program of insurrection among the factory workers.

He did not want a revision of what existed. He did not want a new constitution based on western models. He was convinced that a completely new order was necessary.

Vladimir thought that bits of piecemeal gains and concessions, primarily social and political, slowed the process of achieving the ultimate goal—a classless society. Relatively minor accomplishments like obtaining a constitutional monarchy, improved land distribution, and better working conditions only served to maintain the status-quo and the existing unjust class system. Only with the overthrow of the tsar through class warfare would there be elimination of nobility, bureaucracy, the bourgeoisie, and most of all, capitalism.

In an unsigned essay, "Urgent Tasks of Our Movement," Vladimir outlined the need to have the new Social Democratic party center its mission around a small group of full-time decision-making professional revolutionaries.

Vladimir was concerned that if too many groups or factions became involved, disagreements as to philosophies and strategies would cause the movement to stagnate. He wanted a small tightly knit group of arch-revolutionaries—professionals, not amateurs. Vladimir thought it best to have the revolutionary elite act as the vanguard of the proletariat. This meant that perhaps the leadership would be authoritarian in nature, which at the outset he was willing to accept.

Around 1900 Vladimir began using the pseudonym "Lenin." His writings were read in underground circles and his name was becoming known to revolutionaries and to the police.

Lenin thought that once the Russian Marxists knew how to make a revolution, then it would indeed take place. The time for debate and theory was over, he contended. Besides, the little gains the workers were making by striking would only serve to slow up revolutionary tactics. Something needed to be done quickly.

Lenin came up with an idea to ignite the flames of revolution. An official Social Democrat newspaper published abroad by him and smuggled into Russia would essentially be a "how-to" publication. It would advise the reader as to what steps could be taken, how the many different factions could work together, how to unite for the common cause, and would tell news of the spreading fire of revolution. The paper, appropriately, was to be called *Iskra*—"The Spark."

More than ever, Lenin began to see himself as the practical organizer to carry out the prophecy and spiritual leadership of Karl Marx. And the newspaper, to be controlled by a few dedicated masterminds of the revolution, would be a good practical way of fanning the flames of Marxism in the motherland.

If the revolution needed to be waged like a war, under a unified command, then it was indeed important for Lenin to be stationed at the central command post—not in Siberia. Luckily, the timing for his release, after serving the three years of his exile, could not be better. On February 10, 1900, he set out for European Russia. Krupskaya, on the other hand, needed to remain in Siberia for another year in order to complete her sentence in the town of Ufa, her original destination.

Upon his return from Siberia, the authorities would not permit Lenin to live in St. Petersburg or have contact with certain radicals. He came under the watchful eyes of the police. Therefore he chose to live in the small town of Pskov, a rail junction close to the Latvian border, about a hundred miles from St. Petersburg.

Lenin realized that Pskov would be a good place to have revolutionary literature smuggled into the country. With clever disguises and by resorting to devious routes, he could make regular trips to St. Petersburg with illegal literature. He also was anxious to meet secretly with his fellow revolutionaries in order to boost their sinking morale and to excite them with his plans for *Iskra*. And money for the project had to be raised.

One of the most important persons living in Pskov was a Prince Obolensky. He took a liking to Lenin and was very impressed with his intellect. Normally those sent away to exile were not permitted to have a passport. In order to leave Russia and publish *Iskra* from abroad, Lenin had to have one and, with the prince's influence, he was able to acquire the much-needed document.

He thought that Geneva, Switzerland, a kind of safe haven for many intellectuals and those declared unacceptable by various governments, would be a good place to go. Once again, however, on one of his undercover stays in St. Petersburg, he and his close friend Julius Martov, also recently released from exile, were picked up by the police. The two men were carrying sizeable amounts of money on their persons and were arrested.

After spending a number of hot, miserable weeks in prison, his mother again intervened and was able to get Lenin out of jail. Afterward, he and his mother and sister Anna took a restful river steamer to Ufa, where he was able to bid good-bye to Krupskaya, and then depart for Switzerland. Except for a brief period from 1905 to 1907, Lenin was forced to live in western Europe from 1900 to 1917.

It was apparent that Lenin had gone through a marked change since his last trip abroad. In that five-year period Lenin had emerged as a proven leader, successful organizer, and very productive writer who influenced the thinking of countless readers.

Lenin was being recognized in revolutionary circles as a man who could get the job done as an administrator and activist. Now he was much more confident and assured. He even became forceful enough to disagree and argue with Plekhanov, his former mentor, and other *Iskra* editors. They decided to publish the newspaper in Munich, Germany, where Lenin and his wife Krupskaya, recently freed from exile, moved to direct its operation.

The underground paper *Iskra* (it was once printed in a deeply hidden chamber below the basement of a house) came out once a month. It primarily contained Lenin's views and philosophies. Anyone caught distributing or reading it in Russia was likely to be sent to prison. While living and writing in Germany, Lenin also published an important pamphlet that, along with his provocative *Iskra* articles, revealed much about his strategies. The pamphlet was entitled *What Is To Be Done?*

In *What Is To Be Done?*, published in 1902, Lenin clarified his ideas on revolution and organization. He believed that working-class action would never go beyond the usual techniques used by trade unions to achieve gains. Lenin did not think workers, by themselves, were capable of thinking politically about world wide capitalist issues. He did, however, envisage the potential power of workers in the revolutionary struggle, if correctly guided and motivated.

Lenin also outlined how his party was to be a vanguard, a small, highly compact, disciplined band of professional revolutionaries acting on behalf of the Russian workers. Maximum security against police action was to be maintained. The initiative of the workers was to be controlled and secret terrorist action taken only according to plan. Discussion among the rank and file would not be permitted. One man, or a very small number of men, would make the ultimate decisions. "Give us a handful of revolutionaries and we will overturn Russia," he exclaimed.

In *What Is To Be Done?* Lenin makes an ardent appeal for organization. He points out that the real villains are the bourgeoisie everywhere, not only in Russia. His major idea, or prediction of the future, was that the proletariat of Russia would take power and their lead would be followed by the proletariat of the world. Young intellectuals, an elite full-time core, would be taught to be special assistants to the leaders and would have a much greater involvement in the revolution than "ordinary people."

Lenin also advocated that well-trained revolutionaries should secretly infiltrate the most influential parts of Russian society, every industry, the professions, the church, and even the police and military. By working from within, using propaganda, sabotage, and other techniques, he thought, the mission of overthrowing the autocracy could best be accomplished.

Lenin was continually urging the peasants and workers to rise up against the government, to strike and clash with the police. "To arms, peasants and workers!" he wrote in April 1905.

Lenin implored revolutionaries to build arsenals of rifles, revolvers, bombs, knives, brass knuckles, sticks, rags and kerosene for setting fires, ropes, rope ladders, spades for digging barricades, and barbed wire. He suggested seriously that these weapons be used for killing policemen, blowing up police stations, liberating prisoners, and robbing banks.

In April 1902, despite Plekhanov's wishes for Lenin to return to Switzerland, Lenin, Krupskaya, and most of the editors left Germany and took up residence in London. It seems that the German police, working closely with the Okhrana, were about to close in on the *Iskra* offices in Munich and stop publication. Besides, Lenin reasoned, in England he would be away from his rival, Plekhanov, and his influence. And the paper, he thought, could be put out with lower production costs.

Feeling that he might be followed by Russian agents he took on another new identity, as Jacob Richter, and rented a small apartment-office not far from the British Museum. Like Marx before him, he spent countless mornings reading and researching the many volumes in that great library, never too far afield from his Socialist revolutionary purposes. He loved the place. And in the afternoons he either took English lessons from a tutor in exchange for Russian lessons, supervised the printing of *Iskra*, or met with many of the revolutionaries living in London at that time.

Under the nervous strain of a heavy workload, and being extremely upset over his disputes with Plekhanov, Martov, and other close colleagues, Lenin became quite ill. His body broke out with a severe rash—probably a case of a virus disease called shingles.

By the spring of 1903 it was thought that in the interest of Lenin's health, but more likely because Lenin's adversaries on the editorial board of *Iskra* voted for it, the newspaper was moved to Geneva. Although he had been bedridden, Lenin followed with Krupskaya. They took up residence in a small drab-looking house, using wooden boxes as furniture. It was in a working-class area, perhaps a fitting setting in which to continue the struggle.

In London one autumn morning before their return to Switzerland, Lenin and Krupskaya answered an unexpected knock on their apartment door. A bright-eyed young man of medium build, with thick black wavy hair, introduced himself as a fellow Russian revolutionary. He turned out to be a recent escapee from confinement in Siberia, an émigré, also forced to live outside his native land. Lenin was immediately impressed with his charm, brilliance, and revolutionary record. Though only twenty-two, he was a fearless and ardent activist in the Social Democratic party's underground. When it was discovered that the visitor had earned the nickname of "The Pen" from other revolutionaries for his skill in writing, Lenin became inspired by his presence and at once began to cultivate a professional association with him. The relationship, which lasted for more than two decades, was to become one of great respect coupled with hostility, as so often happens when two strong personalities meet.

The uninvited guest turned out to be Lev Davidovich Bronstein, the son of a Jewish farmer from the Ukraine. He would eventually become a major Soviet political leader under the name of his forged passport: Leon Trotsky. An outstanding theoretician of Marxism, he was a dynamic orator, party organizer, powerful publicist, and writer.

Trotsky had been instrumental in forming the South Russian Workers' Union in 1897. (Unions began to organize in the nineteenth century, but were bitterly fought by employers. In Europe and Russia it was not uncommon for the unions to go on strike and refuse to work until their demands were met.) To further the cause of the union, he edited leaflets and a newspaper, *Our Cause*.

In January 1898, Trotsky had been arrested and two years later sent to Siberia, where he worked as a newspaper columnist. He escaped from Siberia in 1902 and eventually was smuggled out of Russia. In time he was to become a builder of the Red Army during the early stages of its foundation.

Lenin attended his first meeting of the congress of the Social Democratic party in Brussels, Belgium in 1903. Since it was his initial appearance at a congress session, and since he was anxious to convince the delegates that his views were right, he arrived more determined than ever, if not aggressive in mood. Party members would soon take notice of

Lenin. (The Brussels police banned the assembly after it started, forcing it to move to England.)

That congress became the scene of bitter quarreling. Lenin spoke out for his centralized leadership plan outlined in *What Is To Be Done?*, in which everyone would have to follow the leadership. Martov, Trotsky, and Axelrod, his former friends and co-workers on *Iskra*, fearing any form of dictatorship—even a dictatorship of the proletariat—opposed Lenin's concept. They wanted broad input and representation within the party, open to any and all believers.

Two groups were especially dissatisfied with the congress. They were the representatives of the Jewish Socialist branch, an important faction that used democratic procedures to champion the cause of their oppressed people in Poland and Russia, and the Economists.

The Economists were a group whose objective was to improve the condition of life of the working class and to put them in the advance contingent of the people's army—ready, trained, and equipped to bring down the autocracy. Those in opposition to the Economists felt that if economic gains were made by the workers, the revolution might be delayed or never come about at all.

After these two factions walked out of the congress in protest, Lenin, using sharp personal attacks against his adversaries, was able to win his point by a slim voting margin.

Since that time, those who perferred Lenin's approach labeled themselves as Bolsheviks (*bolshoi* means big, or majority), and those who voted in opposition to Lenin as the Mensheviks (*menshie* means small, or minority).

Thus, the battle lines within the movement were drawn, and the debate and infighting would continue for years to come. Many outstanding revolutionaries sided with the Mensheviks, and Lenin became the major flag bearer for the Bolsheviks.

So sure was Lenin that he spoke for most of the Social Democrats that, as exhausted, despondent, and ill as he was after the congress meeting ended in London, he set out to recapture his dominance on the *Iskra* editorial board of directors. But a whispering and gossip campaign of uneasiness about Lenin began to develop. Some of his former friends went so far as to label him a despot. He was soon forced to surrender his role with *Iskra*.

Needing a mental change of pace, he and Krupskaya set out on a month-long hiking tour in the Swiss mountains. They slept outdoors, backpacking along the way.

Somewhat revitalized after his hiking tour, Lenin started a new newspaper called *Vperyod*, meaning "Forward," on January 4, 1905. It was to be a true revolutionary messenger, he announced, not like *Iskra*, the voice of Plekhanov, Martov, and the rest of the minority faction. The title selected may have been a jab at his opponents, for in the spring of 1904 he had written a document against the position of the Mensheviks: *One Step Forward, Two Steps Backward*, subtitled "The Crisis in Our Party." As poor as he and Krupskaya were at this time, he decided to use the meager funds he received from lecturing and from sympathizers like the novelist Maxim Gorky, and went into debt in order to publish *Vperyod*.

Volodya and his sister Olga in Simbirsk

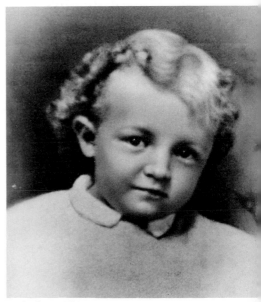

Volodya, 1874

The Ulyanov family, 1879

Nadazhda Krupskaya,
Lenin's wife

Lenin playing chess during
a visit to Maxim Gorky on
Capri

A patrol car in Petrograd, March 2, 1917

Our Newspaper, an organ of the Soviet Workers' and Soldiers' Deputies of the Turkestan area, announcing the victory of revolutionary troops in Petrograd, 1917.

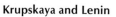

Krupskaya and Lenin

Lenin speaking at the ceremony
unveiling the temporary monument
to Marx and Engels in Revolution
Square, Moscow, on November 7,
1918.

Lenin making a speech in Red Square, Moscow, to commemorate the first May Day in 1919.

Lenin speaking at Sverdlov's funeral in Red Square, 1918

Lenin in the mountains near
Zakopane

Lenin and Krupskaya in their
apartment in the Kremlin,
1920.

Lenin and Stalin in Gorki, 1922

Lenin relaxing in Gorki, 1922

Lenin with members of the St. Petersburg's Union of Struggle for the Emancipation of the Working Class

Chapter 6

A REVOLUTIONARY RETURNS TO RUSSIA

All of Lenin's daily thoughts and activities continued to be directed toward his sole objective in life—to bring about a revolution in Russia. Even his Menshevik opponents admired him for his dedication. Yet for the most part he was on a treadmill, unable to get involved directly and move events toward a showdown.

But all was not at a standstill back home in his native land. A few good things were happening, like the building of the lengthy Trans-Siberian Railway across the entire breadth of Russia toward China and the Pacific Ocean. Industrial output increased, especially in textiles, coal, and metal and iron production. Cotton, minerals, timber, fish, and furs were being exported; however, the workers and peasants received little in return for their long hours of work in the mines, fields, and factories.

In the early 1900s food was relatively scarce since the hard-pressed Russian peasants, with their small plots of land, only did subsistence farming. In addition, the tsar's finance minister, Count Witte, eager to trade surplus grain and foodstuffs abroad for gold, paid little to the farmer for his yields. In order to keep peace in the cities, Minister Witte was interested in seeing that the factory worker wouldn't have to pay too much for his beloved Russian bread. And, when fertilizers for the peasant became too expensive to buy or when drought brought havoc to the farmlands, which was not unusual, peasants and other poor people found it difficult to survive. Thousands died of starvation, epidemics, and malnutrition. On top of that, food riots took the lives of countless others.

Around the turn of the century, the lower classes in Russia felt uncertainty, discontent, and unrest. More than ever, a revolutionary situation began to threaten the tsar. It seemed like the tsar's hold on the people was being shaken.

Strikes, demonstrations, and violent terrorist acts were becoming more frequent. They were not all sponsored by Lenin, but he certainly encouraged such activities. Murders of government officials increased. More and more laws were being broken, leading the police to take harsher measures, often provoking individuals and mobs to attack the uniformed officers.

The tsar at this time was Nicholas II. To add to his woes at home, the Japanese fleet made a surprise attack on the Russian naval vessels stationed on the far eastern coast at Port

Arthur on the Yellow Sea in February 1904. The port was to be connected to the rest of Russia once all the Trans-Siberian tracks were laid. This posed a serious threat to Japan's trade interests and influence in the Far East. Japan had set her sights on Korean and Chinese expansion and she decided to do something about the situation.

Much of Russia's fleet was destroyed. As Japan had British support in the area and the military advantage of fighting close to home, heavy losses were inflicted on Russian military forces. The battles were long and stubborn. Casualties were great on both sides. By the middle of 1905, President Theodore Roosevelt of the United States was able to bring the two warring nations to the peace table, ending the Russo-Japanese War. Tsar Nicholas II began to realize that unless the troops were brought home from the distant front lines of Asia, the Russian empire might crumble from within.

Nicholas and his advisers foresaw that a greater threat might be found closer to his Winter Palace in St. Petersburg, in the rapidly rising hatred and bitterness being shown by his subjects, especially the nearby factory hands. They were flocking to become union members, shouting for more rights and freedom—reforms that the tsar was reluctant to provide. It seemed that Lenin's words were being heeded.

Perhaps Nicholas anticipated that violent days were ahead.

He and his family left for a "vacation" in the south when on Sunday, January 22, 1905, more than 200,000 unarmed workers and their families assembled in the snow near the Winter Palace.

Led by Father Georgi Gapon, a Russian Orthodox priest, they were planning to present a petition to the tsar. They carried ikons and images of the tsar, their beloved father, in a peaceful march, even singing "God Save the Tsar" along the route. The workers belonged to a union organized in 1904 by Father Gapon. They fully expected the tsar to appear in the window of the palace and to acknowledge them with a short speech. Little did they realize that the government was only temporarily tolerant of the newly formed sanctioned unions. The government allowed moderate unions to start only as a means to ward off and weaken the more militant illegal unions, radicals, and revolutionary organizations. Nor did the workers know that government infiltrators had been placed within their ranks to spy on their members.

Alarmed at the size of the crowd, the troopers guarding the palace suddenly opened fire. Then, with sabers swinging mercilessly, the tsar's mounted cossacks rode into the people to disperse them. Hundreds were killed and thousands were wounded. The march was crushed on that "Bloody Sunday," but the revolutionary movement gained sympathy and strength.

Lenin heard of "Bloody Sunday" the next day. At once he and Krupskaya gathered with other Russian revolutionary exiles in Geneva to sing a funeral march to their fallen countrymen. Lenin was wildly excited with the turn of events. Was the long awaited revolution finally underway? Were his dreams, hopes, and everything he worked for about to be realized?

Soon after "Bloody Sunday," Father Gapon, forced to flee Russia, made a dramatic appearance in Geneva. Some of the exiles mistrusted him. Lenin met with the priest, however, and seized upon the idea of having the priest raise funds for weapons to be smuggled to revolutionaries inside Russia. With Lenin's assistance, a shipload of arms and munitions was secretly dispatched to the revolutionaries in order to widen the uprising. Unfortunately for Lenin and his operators, the ship sailing to Russia was driven off course, grounded, and blew up in Finland.

Meanwhile, back in Russia, unrest continued to spread. The masses of people refused the tsar's token attempts to offer political concessions and compromises. Mutinies took place on Russian warships. The army, after suffering defeats in the war with Japan, was demoralized. Hundreds of thousands of workers went out on strike. Peasants burned and looted the estates of their landlords. Noblemen were attacked. There was chaos almost everywhere. Russia was indeed in the throes of a revolution! Lenin was elated.

As soon as the uprising took place, Lenin began to write rousing editorials in *Vperyod* instructing the masses on ways to sabotage, how to participate in street fighting, and techniques of guerrilla warfare. Lenin had always remembered Marx's statement that "Revolutions are the locomotives of history," to which Lenin added his belief that "Revolutions are festivals of the oppressed and the exploited." So after remaining in Switzerland in the months after "Bloody Sunday," Lenin decided that he should come back to Russia and join his countrymen in its struggle.

As the chief strategist of the revolution it was imperative to be in at the beginning. Besides, the tireless Trotsky, his young Menshevik opponent, had already left for Russia and was rapidly gaining respect and power there. Within that year Trotsky was to be elected president of the St. Petersburg Workers Soviet ("soviet" means council, or committee), leading rail and factory workers in massive strikes against the authorities.

In October 1905 Lenin left by train for Stockholm, Sweden, but was delayed there for weeks waiting for a false passport (he was still known to the Russian police as a dangerous revolutionary). After storms further delayed his entry into Russia, Lenin went into hiding, never staying in one house for more than a few days. Later Krupskaya also returned home; however, they usually had to live in different locations.

Lenin's needs and fortunes mirrored the fast-moving events taking place within Russia from 1905 to 1908. During those dynamic days back in his homeland, Lenin was very near to, yet far away from, the action that was taking place. Occasionally he was directly involved in the occurrences, but most often he was forced to be a spectator, viewing proceedings from his hideout just across the border in Kokkola, Finland.

There were times of elation and times of depression. He was often bewildered and dismayed. For one thing, his plan, which he had outlined in *What Is To Be Done?*, to have a small circle of revolutionary leaders control the uprising, was not working out. The Mensheviks were in control. Workers' councils were now representing the masses. Lenin was not being invited to high-level strategy meetings. Some loyalists to the cause began to differ with some of the principles of Karl Marx. Some leading Social Democrats began to question a number of Marxist principles as they applied to Russia and the changes taking place in western European countries. They refused to blindly adhere to the letter of Marx's views.

Once again Lenin's pen became his pistol. This time he was firing at all his opponents, writing bitter articles for a revolutionary paper entitled *Novaya Zhizn*, which means "New Life." The newspaper, supported by the talented writer and friend of the revolutionaries, Maxim Gorky, and published by his common-law wife, was at first a legal Bolshevik publication, but in time it, too, was closed down. All the while the police were in search of Lenin—a prize catch if he could only be found.

The tsar became greatly worried about general strikes, a failing economy, scarcity of food, mass demonstrations, and the fact that armed uprisings broke out in Moscow and several other places. He suddenly agreed to make concessions and bring about reforms. In his October Manifesto, 1905, he publicly promised to give the people more rights, better working conditions, greater freedom, and laws passed only by the Duma, the Russian legislature. Despite the fact that Trotsky denounced the Manifesto and called it a trick to divide the people and break their will to continue the struggle (Lenin agreed), the people accepted the tsar's declaration. They had become too desperate and many among them were still traditional and trusted their tsar.

In a short time, Trotsky was proven right. Seeing that his subjects were returning to their usual apathetic and obedient ways, the tsar permitted the "Black Hundreds," bands of heavily armed, superpatriots, to seek out scapegoats, minority groups, and strikers. Almost anyone opposed to the regime was fair game. Thousands were brutally assaulted, robbed, firebombed, and murdered. Revenge was the motive of these ruthless gangs. Hardly anyone who had ever dissented could be considered safe from harm. And the tsar's officials took charge again. Arrests were rampant and included Trotsky and all the leaders of the St. Petersburg Soviet. One of the reasons for the failure of the St. Petersburg Soviet was that its leaders couldn't coordinate their actions with the Moscow Soviet, in spite of Lenin's urgings.

Lenin had little choice but to be more of an observer than an operator. He would have loved to be a manager, rather than a monitor. And as the year 1905 ended, the back of the workers revolt in St. Petersburg was broken. The final blow was delivered in the Presnaya district of Moscow. The start of a peaceful strike there turned into nine days of fierce street fighting, pitting workers, women, and children against ten thousand police and government troops. The squads of guerrillas, behind every kind of street barricade imaginable, with only a few hundred small arms at their disposal, battled the tsar's soldiers and their tremendous firepower. In the end, courage, cobblestones, and snipers' bullets were no match for machine guns and cannons. The mutiny of the troops anticipated by the street fighters never happened.

The Moscow revolution failed for a number of reasons. It started slowly, developed sporadically, and then grew in size and intensity. It was an ill-prepared spontaneous uprising, without plan, discipline, or goal. The army and navy remained loyal to the tsar. News of the uprising spread too slowly. There was lack of unity between peasant and worker, as well as between the Bolsheviks and Mensheviks.

The uprising had violated all of the principles Lenin had set down as being necessary for a successful revolution. In fact, Lenin had written to members of the Moscow Soviet from his refuge in Finland telling them it wasn't time yet for the revolution. Nevertheless, Lenin praised this heroic attempt of the working class very highly. He considered the Revolution of 1905 the "dress rehearsal" for the future revolution in Russia.

For the next year and a half a forlorn and discouraged Lenin moved about between Moscow, St. Petersburg, and Finland. He left once in 1906 to attend the Stockholm unification congress in Sweden. He continued to write anonymous pamphlets, urging the people to rise up once more against the authorities.

In 1907 Lenin left Moscow to attend the Congress of the United party held in London. Once there, he continued his argumentative speeches against Leon Trotsky (who had since escaped from another imprisonment in Siberia) and his Menshevik followers.

It was at the congress that he became acquainted with a young dark-skinned supporter from Georgia, a southern region of Russia, named Joseph Dzhugashvili. The world would later come to know him as Joseph Stalin, which means "man of steel." Stalin lived up to his name by ruling the Soviet Union with an iron fist from 1929 until his death in 1953.

After he returned from London, Lenin realized that his stay in Russia was becoming increasingly risky. He decided to leave once again for Finland. But he could never be secure about his refuge in Finland, or his safe houses in Russia. His many disguises, which included a beardless face, a mustache clipped short, wigs, and frequent changes of hats, were effective, but no guarantee that he would not be detected.

Toward the end of the year Lenin suddenly decided to depart for Sweden, hoping to book passage on a steamer. Since the secret police almost always sought suspects at railroad terminals, Lenin cautiously left the train before it was to arrive in Abo, the point of his embarkation by sea.

Lenin's escape plan called for boarding the boat at an island stopover, three miles from Abo. It was a dangerous shortcut, a route taken across a frozen inlet in bitter cold weather. Relying on two local Finnish peasants who were supposed to know the ice conditions, all three men nearly lost their lives. It seems that the drunken guides became somewhat confused and followed a path that took them onto thin ice. The ice cracked and gave way. Miraculously all three were saved and Lenin caught his boat just in time.

Lenin in one of his many disguises, 1917

Chapter 7

RUMORS, RIFTS, AND RHETORIC

Leaving his country once again to settle in other European countries was for Lenin akin to a second emigration. As fate would have it, almost a decade would pass before he could return to Russia in 1917. During this period Lenin was often pessimistic. He feared Bolshevism would never change the destiny of Russia.

Lenin's moods could be especially low and his frustrations frequent. A new prime minister, P.A. Stolypin, had been chosen in 1906. He allowed limited gains for the workers and peasants, which defused the revolutionary fervor. Indifference and inertia prevailed among the Russian people.

To add to Lenin's despondency, many other problems affected him as well. Lenin was not in the best of health, suffering from bouts with stomach disorders, insomnia, and headaches, all attributed to tension and stress. But Krupskaya and her mother, of whom he was very fond, kept nursing his body and mind as best they could. On more than one occasion they prescribed rest and diversion for him in order to prevent a nervous breakdown.

Upon reestablishing residence in a run-down section of Geneva in 1908, Lenin found life there to be rather dull and uninspiring. Many of his Social Democrat friends, always on hand for a stimulating discussion, had abandoned him in favor of a more independent life. He studied in the library whenever he could, and at night he and Krupskaya most often went to the movies or the theater for diversion. But undoubtedly their minds were usually elsewhere.

Early in 1909 Lenin, his wife, mother-in-law, and sister Maria moved to Paris. Despite the poor state of their finances, the four rented a roomy and bright apartment on a nice residential street. Lenin's luck failed to improve in Paris. The national library refused him the privilege of borrowing books. He absent-mindedly had a series of bicycle accidents and one time his bike was stolen, further complicating his ability to go places and do things.

In Paris more of his colleagues deserted him and the number of his enemies seemed to be increasing. At a meeting of the Socialist International held in Copenhagen in 1910, Lenin was attacked and blamed by many of those in attendance for bringing disunity to the movement. His popularity was at its lowest ebb. When he returned to Paris shortly thereafter, a dissenting group of troublemakers raided a cafe where Lenin and other Bolsheviks had gathered. A wild fight began. Lenin was present during the brawl, but escaped without injury. These situations caused him further dejection.

Though Lenin was outwardly very proper about his personal conduct—he did not smoke and rarely drank anything except a little wine and dark beer—many of his associates, and especially those in the camp of the opposition, indulged in idle talk about his private life. For many years two rumors persisted throughout Europe that may have been well founded. One topic involved his close friendship and feeling for an attractive young woman active in Bolshevik affairs. The other gossip focused on the suspicion that Lenin and his party cronies were recipients of illegal funds obtained from secret sources inside Russia.

Lenin's infatuation with Inessa Armand, a strikingly attractive Parisian-born mother of five children and the former wife of a wealthy Moscow manufacturer, began with their meeting in the French capital in 1910. For many years she and the famous Bolshevik leader were romantically linked. Inessa was no ordinary woman. She was very lively, intelligent, and had a youthful if not pretty face. Her features were accented by thick, chestnut-colored hair and alluring eyes.

Lenin was greatly impressed with Inessa's versatility. She played the piano excellently, was well versed in classical music, and was fluent in four languages. Along with Lenin, she taught a course on political economy for Russian émigrés at a school started by Lenin and Krupskaya on the outskirt of Paris. But especially gratifying to Lenin was the fact that Inessa had carried out missions for the Bolsheviks inside Russia. She was arrested there twice and had escaped from a two-year exile in Siberia.

The amazing part of Lenin's relationship with the glamorous Inessa was that Krupskaya knew that the two had romantic feelings toward one another, yet she liked Inessa and accepted the situation. She offered to divorce Lenin but he would not hear of it. Apparently he had a different kind of affection for Krupskaya, built on respect, loyalty, and companionship over the years.

Lenin and Inessa remained very close friends. She even moved to Cracow, Poland, in 1912, and Berne, Switzerland, in 1914, to be near Lenin and his wife when they established residences in those cities. In the meantime, Inessa carried out many important assignments for Lenin and accompanied him on the dramatic train ride back to Russia in 1917.

Another matter of great discussion and concern among the party members was the questionable activities of the partisans, the devoted followers of the Bolsheviks and Mensheviks. These devotees were officially condemned by the Stockholm congress for their method of obtaining illegal money. It was said that they often resorted to forging banknotes, obtaining gifts via suspicious circumstances through the wills of rich businessmen, and staged a number of bank holdups. Even Joseph Dzhugashvili was a suspect in one robbery that took place in Georgia. Many of the more idealistic revolutionaries criticized these practices and charged Lenin with approval of and complicity in the wrongdoings.

By 1912 the Bolsheviks and Mensheviks had acquired a degree of legal recognition as offshoots of the Social Democratic party, now represented in the Duma. The two factions held thirteen seats in the Parliament, although the Duma had little power to override the wishes of the tsar's ministers. One of the Bolsheviks elected was Roman Malinovsky, a man closely allied to Lenin. Lenin used him to prevent the Menshevik position from achieving status in the Duma. Only the Bolshevik position was to be promoted, and Malinovsky's job was to prevent any unification of the two factions from taking place. Lenin was delighted with his work in keeping the groups apart.

In 1913, Lenin set out on a campaign to capture the editorial board of *Pravda*, the popular, pro-Socialist newspaper of Russia. With the use of his three young agents, Jacob Sverdlov, Lev Kamenev, and Joseph Dzhugashvili, he cleverly had one of his most influential supporters, Miron Chernomazov, appointed editor-in-chief of the paper. His objective was to destroy the credibility of the Mensheviks and win more adherents to the Bolsheviks' side.

His delight with the *Pravda* coup suddenly turned into a

disaster. Sverdlov and Dzhugashvili, previously on the police wanted list, were arrested and sent to Siberia. But Kamenev escaped the police roundup. Then in the following weeks other inside agents, their identities known only to Malinovsky and a few "trusted" inside operators, were arrested also.

Critics of Lenin had been saying that he was a poor judge of men and could readily be misled. This time his adversaries were right. He really was duped. Not only was it discovered that Chernomazov was a paid police agent, but Malinovsky, one of Lenin's most faithful long-time comrades in Bolshevik inner circles, was shockingly unmasked as a high-ranking Russian secret police agent.

Now the Mensheviks and other Social Democrats, many of whom had been suspicious about Malinovsky right along, saw Lenin and his Bolsheviks as gullible. Lenin's reputation in the Socialist International was practically ruined.

From 1907 until World War I, Lenin lost the support and friendship of much of the Bolshevik intelligentsia. It seems that a mood of contemplation and soul-searching suddenly came upon the more learned and articulate liberals of society. They began speculating about philosophy, human psychology, aesthetics, and morals. They were now directing their minds toward a metaphysical understanding of the revolution.

The switch in focus at that time dealt with the question of what was real, the existence of God, and such abstract thoughts as the explanation, nature, character, and causes of being and knowing. Many of the great thinkers of this movement—even some Bolsheviks—became more concerned with the spiritual emancipation of humans and lifting the dignity of man, than in ways to make a revolution. This departure disturbed Lenin very much.

During Lenin's most trying years abroad, despite the many setbacks he encountered with friends and opponents alike, he never deviated from or compromised his major Marxist principles. At times, though, as a realist, he was compelled to bend a bit on practical matters. Nevertheless, though often isolated, he stood his ground against the new Bolshevik philosophers, men like Alexander Bogdanov, a brilliant writer and former aide of Lenin, and others who differed from his ideologies and approaches.

Wherever Lenin went, be it a congress meeting of Social Democrats in some European city, an informal gathering of intelligentsia, or editorial board policy meetings, those who would stand in the way of the revolutionary cause, no matter how liberal the issue, would come under Lenin's wrath.

Those who wanted unity with the hated Mensheviks, whether anyone in his own ranks or in the various splinter groups who became soft on revolution, were seen as "liquidators." Lenin gave that name to anyone who he thought was helping to kill the radical tactics of the party. He even went so far as to advocate that they be expelled from active membership.

Barricades in Petrograd, February 1917

Chapter 8

WORLD WAR I

On June 28, 1914, on a street in Sarajevo, Bosnia, in what is now central Yugoslavia, Archduke Francis Ferdinand, heir-apparent to Franz Joseph's throne of Austria-Hungary, was assassinated by a Serbian young man. Within a month and a half, all of Europe was at war.

Lenin was aware that Franz Joseph, the ruler of the Austro-Hungarian Empire, and Tsar Nicholas II of Russia were both anxious to expand their national interests in the troubled Balkans, but he never expected the two powers to go to war over the territory. "A war between Austria and Russia would be a very useful thing for the revolution," Lenin had written Gorky in 1913, "but it's not likely that Franz Joseph and Nicky will give us the pleasure."

Perhaps because Lenin was too involved with his revolutionary aspirations and his problem in obtaining expense money, he was not alert immediately to the beneficial possibilities of the current situation. When war did break out in

August 1914, he was actually in Vienna. The Austrian authorities immediately rounded up all Russians as enemy aliens; Lenin was imprisoned for twelve days until they became convinced that he was a notorious enemy of the tsar, and released him.

Lenin and his wife settled in Berne, Switzerland, a city relatively inexpensive for living, in a country that remained neutral throughout the conflict. Now Lenin became a very interested bystander to all the wartime happenings. He realized each event had great meaning for the revolution.

For the Russian government, the outlook for winning the war was bleak, right from the start. Russia signed treaties to join forces with France and England, who more or less owned three-quarters of all foreign investments in Russia. This strange alignment of nations was called the "Triple Entente." These three powers were pitted against the "Triple Alliance," consisting of Germany, Austria-Hungary, and Turkey, which had a lesser role. These partners were known also as the Central Powers. Late in the war, the United States sent troops to France and fought as an ally of England and France.

At the outset Lenin had reasoned that with most of Europe's countries at war, and with the armies at the front, workers of all nations would soon realize that their tragedies and sufferings were brought on by selfish capitalist interests powerful enough to gain control of the ruling circles.

Then, he thought, the hand of Socialists everywhere would be strengthened and revolutions would begin across national borders. Lenin miscalculated. The reverse took place. National loyalties, expressed even by Socialists in their respective countries, took precedence over all other considerations. Patriotic feelings ran high. Surprisingly, young Marxists demonstrating their love of country rushed to sign up for military service.

Lenin was confounded by the rash of nationalism being shown. He felt betrayed. What was happening to the international commitment to socialism? Even the highly regarded Georgi Plekhanov was supporting the Allies against Germany. Once again, Lenin stood alone on an issue and publicly denounced all who disagreed with him. And they in turn jeered and mocked Lenin each and every time he would speak out against assistance for the Russian war effort. He became so angry that he seriously proposed that the new revolutionary slogan become "Turn your guns on your officers!"

In the spring of 1915, Krupskaya's mother died and Lenin was grief stricken. Then a second period of deep sorrow afflicted him fourteen months later when he learned of his own mother's death. He agonized greatly over both of these losses. Lenin was emotionally close to both women. His mother, even in her last years, continued to support him morally and helped with his financial difficulties whenever she could. She had stood by him in every crisis.

By 1916 he was again in a state of remorse and despair. Lenin felt that his life as an exile would never end. He wondered if the revolution would ever come about in his lifetime. And to compound his feelings of futility, he was still unable to win over comrades to his positions. He was unpopular and he knew it. However, with few victories and many defeats, Lenin still managed to stand firm behind his convictions.

For Russia at war also, victories were all too few and defeats were staggering. In the fall of 1914 a series of military blunders by Russian generals in East Prussia led to a major loss on the battlefield. At Tannenberg over 100,000 Russians were captured and tens of thousands were killed and wounded.

In later fighting against the Germans and Austrians, despite the great courage exhibited by the tsar's troops, there were about thirty thousand casualties each day. Planning was bad. With a broken-down railway system, the troops did not have adequate supplies. Reverses and retreats began to wear on the suffering Russian soldiers. Countless numbers surrendered or deserted from their outfits.

The situation became so bad by the fall of 1915 that Tsar Nicholas, succumbing to pressure and bad advice, took personal command of the armies in the field. Nicholas was no help to his faltering army. To make matters worse, in his absence the running of the government was left to his wife, the German-born Tsarina Alexandra, who was under the hypnotic spell of a strange monk from Siberia named Grigori Yefimovich Rasputin.

Rasputin had won the favor of Alexandra, but most Russians feared and hated him. It seems that Rasputin was able to convince the tsarina that he had mystical powers to heal her little son, Alexis, of his hemophilia. Rasputin, usually dirty and drunk, shrewdly influenced Alexandra to make important decisions, even dismissing and appointing high-ranking ministers of the government. Scandal and shame struck the palace.

As Rasputin's power over Alexandra, and therefore Nicholas, grew, the people began to lose their respect for and confidence in the imperial couple. Nicholas was far removed from what was happening around him and the spreading discontent in the cities and countryside. Disorders were growing. The number of war dead continued to mount. Anti-German feeling ran high. The German-sounding name of St. Petersburg was changed to Petrograd. The incidence of arrests and assassinations skyrocketed. And on a cold night in December 1916, Rasputin, who some thought was a secret German agent, met a predictable fate. At a palace party he was poisoned, shot, and while still alive, dumped into the icy Neva River and left there to die.

With the war just about lost, with Rasputin, the power

behind the throne, out of the way, and with the Duma doing little to satisfy the needs of the people, the revolutionaries and others opposed to the government began to take matters into their own hands. The people had had their fill of wars, strikes, demonstrations, food lines, looting, riots, and bloodshed. By 1917 they also had their fill of the autocratic Romanovs, the family of tsars who had ruled Russia for three hundred years.

When riots broke out in Petrograd during early March 1917, Nicholas II ordered troops sent there to restore order. It was too late. Mobs ran rampant. The soldiers refused to fire on the crowds of strikers and demonstrators. Many troop units supported the rioters. The government resigned, and the Duma, supported by the army, called upon the tsar to give up his throne. He and his family were immediately arrested and later sent to Siberia, a destiny that he had ordered for thousands of others. About a year later Nicholas and his family were murdered in the house in which they were being held prisoners.

A provisional government was formed to take over. It immediately enacted a number of liberal and permissive laws, abolishing the police and replacing them by a people's militia. With the sudden arrival of freedom of speech and other new-found rights, the country rapidly fell into a state of anarchy.

The Russian Revolution of 1917 is generally regarded as

one of the great episodes in world history. Few leaders, including the tsar and Lenin himself, anticipated that the revolution would occur when it did. Just a few weeks before the revolution began, while speaking to a group of young Swiss laborers and regretting that his moment may never come, Lenin declared: "We, the old ones, may never live to see the decisive battles of the coming revolution."

In the weeks following the fall of the tsar, Lenin devoured every bit of news from his homeland. Sometimes the stories he received were conflicting and confusing. He was especially worried that some other insurgent group, or the Duma, with their own form of government, would oust the provisional government before he was able to be on the scene to direct the Bolsheviks' quest for power.

Political prisoners were rapidly being released from exile in Siberia. Stalin, Martov, and other Bolsheviks raced to their action stations in Petrograd, and Trotsky was en route home from Canada. But an almost insurmountable predicament was confronting Lenin. How could he safely return to Russia as soon as possible to take charge of the revolution? Germany and Russia were still at war and getting through the war zone would be nearly impossible. After all, with things so unsettled at home, and with so much distrust for the Bolsheviks the world over, Lenin could easily become an assassin's target anywhere, at any time.

A solution was found. A secret plan was worked out whereby Lenin would be allowed to pass through Germany to Sweden in a "sealed" railway car. It was called sealed because Lenin and his party were not allowed to get off at stops. Then he and other exiles accompanying him could proceed to Petrograd via Finland. It was in Germany's interest to provide safe passage to Lenin. Since Lenin and his comrades were in favor of ending the war, the advantage to Germany would be great. The German generals could, with war-weary Russia out of the war, concentrate on defeating the Allies on the western front. Besides, it was assumed that Lenin, upon his return, would further divide and weaken the newly established provisional government with his dramatic appeal to the masses to fight for "peace, bread, and freedom." Sometimes that rallying slogan was changed to a cry for "peace, land, bread, and power." Lenin wanted it all for the people.

The provisional government that ran Russia after the tsar was toppled proved to be rather weak. It did, however, pledge to continue the war. The leaders felt that if Russia remained loyal to her democratic allies—England and France in particular—she would be rewarded after the war ended.

All kinds of investments, loans, and assistance would be needed to make the country self-sufficient. This reasoning was based on the fact that beyond the political revolution taking place inside Russia, a rapidly developing industrial revolution also was spreading throughout the world. If living standards were to be raised and democracy was to survive under the new order, Russia would need to become an industrial power.

When Lenin learned about the first provisional government, the name of its foremost leader immediately rang a bell. It was Alexander Kerensky, none other than the son of the former headmaster of his hometown school in Simbirsk. Kerensky, a young leader of the Socialist wing of the Duma, was more moderate in philosophy than Lenin. With his handsome features, law background, and fiery manner of speech, he had attracted a large group of supporters. Kerensky, like Lenin, was extremely energetic and capable. They were soon to become bitter rivals in the events that made up the October Revolution.

Not long after the formation of the provisional government, Victor Chernov, a Menshevik member of its administration, harshly criticized Lenin by implying that, despite his great abilities, he lacked direction because he had been away from events at home and forced to live underground for so many years. Upon hearing the charge against him, Lenin replied in his own biting way, "I may not know where I am going, but I am going there with determination."

Lenin indeed knew where he was going—to Petrograd—and he was determined to get there as quickly as possible.

Lenin was extremely excited about the train ride home.

Even the presence of an angry crowd of pro-war, anti-Bolshevik Russians gathered at the Berne railway station to jeer could not dampen the spirits of Lenin and the thirty exiles in his party. When the departing group was insulted with cries of "German spies" and curses, Lenin and his followers began to sing the "Internationale," the emotional anthem of the revolutionary movement. Fistfights broke out. Then the train pulled out of the station, and Lenin, true to form, went to his compartment and started to work on his papers.

Chapter 9

LENIN RETURNS AGAIN

The train took four days to get out of Germany. Lenin, a shut-in for the entire time, grew impatient with the slow pace of the journey. Once in Sweden and then in Finland, as he came closer and closer to his homeland, his feeling of anticipation accelerated. Now almost forty-seven years old, Lenin wondered what was in store for him. Would the provisional government have him arrested? Would he have to go into hiding again? Who would be at the station to greet him? How would he be received? Was he remembered?

Lenin should have had some inkling as to what would happen. But he didn't. At a stopover in Sweden a group of Swedish Social Democrats, aware of his presence, sponsored a "coming out" party for him. At the border between Finland and Russia, he was pleasantly surprised by a large contingent of workmen at the station cheering him on with loud chants of "Le-nin! Le-nin!" He was given a large bouquet of red roses. But, as he and his fellow travelers pulled into the Finland Station in Petrograd after 11:00 P.M. on the night of April 16, 1917, a reception befitting a conquering hero awaited him.

The emotional outpouring of people was spectacular. Many hundreds of supporters and admirers were on hand to welcome him home. Home at last! There were ordinary Bolsheviks, workers' delegations, troops from a nearby fortress, local soldiers, an honor guard, and leaders of the Petrograd soviet, most with banners and signs wildly shouting their greetings and slogans. Speeches were given. A band played. There was marching. Searchlights from the Fortress of Peter and Paul were beamed onto the platform. The celebration was to last for a half hour before a shocked Lenin was whisked away to the former tsar's private waiting room in the railway station. Of all places! He must have thought about all his years of waiting.

Outside the station more crowds waited to hail Lenin. Thousands were in the streets. They wanted more than a glimpse of him. They had read his written words. Now they wanted to hear him. Lenin obligingly climbed on the hood of an armored car (now a national monument on display in Leningrad with the inscription, "Long Live the Socialist Revolution") and with a fervent speech made a plea for the start of a worldwide Socialist revolution. Then, while proceeding toward the newly seized palacelike headquarters of the Bolsheviks (formerly the estate of the tsar's favorite ballerina), Lenin's procession was held up at practically every intersection. More crowds awaited him! He was unable to continue until each audience heard his voice with reassurances that better days were ahead.

All through the night, Lenin, with a recharged burst of energy and exuberance, addressed the hundreds of party leaders and workers who had anxiously waited for him at the headquarters estate. One of his speeches lasted ninety minutes. Then he would repeatedly go to the upper balcony outside the large mansion and lecture the triumphant throngs below. His words were candid, if not startling, for the many who heard his message. That night and in the weeks and months ahead, all of the country would be roused by what Lenin had to say.

When all the uproar ended in the wee hours of the morning, Lenin finally managed a broad smile. His expressive face revealed his pleasure with the turn of events. Then he and Krupskaya were taken to the apartment of his sister Anna and her husband Mark. Maria, his unmarried sister, was also present for the heartwarming reunion, after which Lenin was able to get some rest. As the first order of business the next day, Lenin went to the cemetery to pay his respects to his mother. At her grave he paused and reflected about the meaning of her life, their mutual love, and all that had transpired in his life.

When the celebrations were over, the job of getting on

with the formation of the new order of things began to demand attention. Lenin wanted to change things around quickly and radically. The Bolsheviks were to be called Communists, and the ministers would be renamed commissars. He advocated that the regional people's councils, or soviets, should draft new laws. "All power to the soviets" was his often repeated slogan. He rallied the peasants to the idea of seizing land from the landowners. It was justified, he exclaimed. He spoke out for the war to end, but defeats continued. And more than anything else, he harangued about the ineptitude of the provisional government—how slowly it moved and how poorly it was operating. Lenin warned that lawlessness would result in Russia if the government continued in power. Turmoil would be terrible.

Adding to the confusion were the eighteen different organized revolutionary groups that were extant in Russia in 1917. Lenin felt that there was entirely too much arguing going on. He had no faith in the Duma—a debating society he thought—or any form of parliamentary government. He would have to take matters into his own hands. It was time for action. It was time for an armed insurrection. It was time for Lenin to plan Kerensky's downfall.

By the middle of July, anti-government propaganda by the Bolsheviks began to take its toll in Petrograd. Thousands of inflammatory placards like "War to the Palaces; Peace to the Huts" were posted about the city. Demonstrations and mass marches were becoming very disorderly. Crowds of workers and servicemen roamed the streets. Rumors and riots replaced reasoning. One rumor had it that twenty thousand sailors had mutinied and were on their way to join the mobs. When large numbers of government troops, mostly loyal soldiers, were dispatched to confront the mobs, bloody clashes took place and the crowds were dispersed. It was an ugly scene.

The Bolsheviks were accused of treason. Leon Trotsky, a powerful public orator, now back home and working closely with Lenin, was placed under arrest along with other high-ranking revolutionaries and hundreds of others. Lenin was resting at a cottage at a Finnish resort town at the time. Nevertheless, he was immediately accused of acting as a German spy. The government produced documents—later shown to be forgeries—stating that the Bolsheviks had received money from the Germans to carry on activities that would bring down the current administration.

Now the provisional government had a warrant out to arrest him on sight. They blamed him for inciting the riots and planning a revolution. Worst of all he was, they said, a foreign agent, an enemy of the state.

Lenin's friends dissuaded him from giving himself up in order to stand trial. Perhaps it would be good for the cause, he thought, if he became a martyr. He was now a fugitive. Once again he had to resort to clever methods of evasion, many of which were used successfully over the years. He now had to travel with bodyguards. Secret routes for getting around had to be laid out.

Over the years Lenin had become a master at hiding secret papers in the under-sole of his boots or shoes. He devised ingenious ways to build secret drawers under chessboard tables or to conceal papers in books and false-bottom trunks. He always used fictitious names and illegal identity papers. He could readily disguise himself as a peasant or worker. Good wigs were constantly available for him. One time while hiding in Finland, he feigned being unable to hear or speak. Another time he appeared on a Petrograd streetcar, his face covered with a huge wraparound bandage. When one lady asked him if he was going to the big demonstration at the Smolny, the Bolsheviks headquarters (which was precisely where he was headed), he responded by telling her that his jaw was swollen and he was going to the dentist.

The dragnet for the main Bolshevik leader continued. Lenin was out of sight, but not out of mind. People wondered about his whereabouts. Unverified reports claimed that he had said his good-bye to Krupskaya and had fled the country in a German submarine. In reality he had been smuggled out of Petrograd in a freight train to a small village. There he shaved off his beard and lived in a field hut alongside a lake. His desk and chair were two tree stumps. He was forced to survive on a diet of tea and potatoes cooked over a fire.

Late in August, with cold weather setting in, Lenin was forced to escape to Finland. Since the border checkpoints were heavily guarded, Lenin and his contacts had to come up with a very adroit method of avoiding detection. With the help of sympathetic railway workers, Lenin was passed off as a stoker tending the fire of the steam engine of a locomotive. Once in Finland, he found work as a farmer. Then later fantastic plans for Lenin's safety and protection were made.

In order for Lenin to continue with his writings (he wrote sixty-five articles and letters in hiding) and underground activities, he had to be in a city. Secret messages had to be sent by trusted couriers and cryptic telegrams and letters had to be dispatched quickly. In Helsinki, there were many secret agents and Bolshevik supporters. One such man was Gustav Rovio, none other than the chief of police of that Finnish capital. Who would ever suspect that he would provide the safest haven of all for Lenin—an apartment in his own home? And that is precisely what he did.

Each day Lenin was away from the fast-moving events in Petrograd, he became more on edge. Eschewing the danger, he urgently sought permission of the government in power to return home. But they forbade him to do so. In the meantime the provisional government's situation was going from bad to worse. Their recognition and acceptance remained weak after the July uprising. Prince Lvov, the prime minister, resigned. Kerensky still refused to sue for peace. As war losses mounted, army support weakened. The Germans were threatening Petrograd. Russia was powerless. There was further economic deterioration and the prices of goods and food grew practically out of reach.

During these very difficult days General Lavr Kornilov was appointed commander in chief of the army with the hope that he might be able to bring order and stability to the desperate situation. At the outset it seemed he was an ideal choice. Kornilov was a conservative military man who wanted to preserve established traditions. He resisted change. He was regarded as honest, courageous, and intensely patriotic. Yet politically he proved to be naive, too trustworthy of the words and promises of politicians. Politics confused him. When he sought immediate permission of the provisional government to tighten discipline at the front that included restoring the death penalty for breaking ranks, or for other unsoldierlike actions, and other reforms, it took weeks before Kerensky acted. When the two fought openly about what needed to be done, General Kornilov was dismissed.

In September General Kornilov, a staunch conservative, tried to topple the provisional government by ordering his army to march on Petrograd, but this failed. Many of his soldiers, unwilling to fire on their "brothers," either the loyalist forces of the government or the heavily armed Bolsheviks, deserted the ranks. Thousands of soldiers went over to the side of the Bolsheviks who welcomed their weapons and military know-how. Now the Bolsheviks, in control of the Petrograd soviet and with a Trotsky-organized militia of twenty-five thousand (soon to become the Red Guard) ready to flex their muscles, needed Lenin's leadership more than ever.

Petrograd, October 26, 1917—Forward, to the Winter Palace!

Chapter 10

THE OCTOBER REVOLUTION:
SHOTS HEARD AROUND THE WORLD

The revolutionary flag was raised over the palace of the tsars on October 26, 1917. The Bolsheviks referred to the series of events of that time as the "Great October Socialist Revolution." The revolution actually took place on October 25, 1917, according to the Russian calendar in effect then. That is why it is often called the October Revolution by the Russians. According to the western calendar, the day was November 7. (A decree by Lenin replaced the old Julian calendar with the Gregorian calendar, common throughout the western world. The Julian calendar had been two weeks behind the Gregorian, or new-style, calendar now being used.) That explains why the rebellion is also known as the November Revolution. Sometimes it is labeled the Bolshevik Revolution as well.

John Reed, the American journalist who was an eyewitness to the historical episodes of that fall, called his account of the revolution *Ten Days That Shook the World*. Though many people were instrumental in bringing about the revolution, Lenin was the major force.

Lenin, charged with the responsibility of running a nation for the first time, was faced with the perplexing problems common to most great leaders in their initial courses of action. Lenin was constantly confronted with the dilemma of when to remain idealistic and when to employ pragmatic solutions that might be counter to the philosophy of socialism.

The power that Lenin exercised as supreme ruler was never utilized for himself. All his decisions, it seems, were based on a determination of what was right for the young country in its early years of struggles.

On the night of the uprising, Lenin was still hiding out in a friend's apartment in the suburbs of Petrograd. Kerensky had ordered troops into the city. Telephone lines for the Smolny Institute, taken over as command headquarters by Trotsky and his Bolshevik Red Guards, were cut. Bolshevik printing plants were smashed by the government to prevent the printing of inflammatory literature. With these precautions taken, the government expected to crush any uprising.

By making the first move, Kerensky played into Trotsky's hands. Now the people could be told that the Bolsheviks had to act in self-defense. But in reality, Trotsky and his officers had taken the offensive days before. A brilliant plan to capture Petrograd with a minimum of casualties was under way.

Finally, Lenin could wait no longer. Wearing a skillfully contrived disguise, he boarded the last streetcar of the night and headed for the Smolny. He arrived undetected amid a hubbub of activity and immediately took charge.

At the Smolny just before daybreak, Lenin gave the order to attack. All the ten major drawbridges over the Neva River, the telegraph office, telephone exchange, railway stations, and power plants were taken in quick bold moves. This isolated the government's palace strongholds, causing operations to come to a standstill. No troops could be called up, since it was now impossible to send orders to army garrisons outside Petrograd. Those army bases inside the city had already been "Bolshevized" by infiltrators and barrages of propaganda. As soon as the clashes and skirmishes started, thousands of soldiers and sailors left their posts and went over to the side of the Bolshevik forces.

Everything went according to plan. At 9:40 P.M. the Russian cruiser *Aurora* fired the first shot that signaled the rebel charge to the gates on the Winter Palace. The small defending detachment of military cadets, 170 uniformed women soldiers, and cossacks were hardly a match for the 50,000 Red Guards, former servicemen, and all kinds of rebel units massed outside to storm the palace. They had little difficulty entering the darkened building.

Within five hours the frightened government ministers and officials hiding inside the magnificent residence were rounded up and arrested. They had expected Kerensky to rally loyal troops stationed outside Petrograd for a counterattack. That never happened. Kerensky, disguised and supplied with a fast car by the American Embassy, slipped out of the palace unnoticed and escaped to the United States.

Lenin, true to his character, allowed himself little time to savor the victory. He rose early the next morning after a few hours of restless sleep and immediately got to the task of drafting decrees to be submitted to the new Bolshevik governing body called the Council of People's Commissars. Lenin became its chairman: in effect, the prime minister. That evening he presented his decrees to a wildly cheering and approving session of the Congress of Soviets. They called for a peace settlement and the abolishment of private land ownership.

John Reed, present at the assembly that night, offered this description of Lenin: a "short, stocky figure, with a big head set down in his shoulders, bald and bulging. Little eyes, a snubbish nose, with wide generous mouth, and heavy chin; clean-shaven now, but already beginning to bristle with the well-known beard of his past and future. Dressed in shabby clothes, his trousers much too long for him."

Then when he rose to speak, Reed's account continues, he gripped the "edge of the reading stand, letting his little wrinkling eyes travel over the crowd as he stood there waiting, apparently oblivious to the long-rolling ovation, which lasted several minutes. Then in a very matter of fact tone said, 'We shall now proceed to construct the Socialist order!'"

The October Revolution had ended. In many respects it was a silent revolution, with relatively little bloodshed. Although it was of short duration, it had been very long in the making. Its rumblings were heard around the globe. Practically overnight Russia and communism became perceived as a potential threat by the capitalist nations of the west. And the founder of the Soviet Union, Lenin, became famous with his rise to power.

Lenin presiding at a sitting of the Soviet of People's Commissars in Moscow, October 1919.

May Day, 1919

Chapter 11

WAR AND PEACE

Lenin soon found out that it was a lot easier to be the architect of the new social order than its builder. Adjustments and changes in the original blueprint had to be made along the way. Knowledgeable and cooperative workmen were not always available. Vital materials were often in short supply. And certain disruptive forces did everything they could to prevent the erection of the structure as it was beginning to take form.

Lenin saw to it that there would be a newly written Soviet constitution. It appeared on July 10, 1918. New laws and many radical changes were established, followed by decree after decree. Most of the country's privately owned industries, banks, mines, land, and property were put under the ownership or control of the national government. Foreign trade also was nationalized. Workers were required to work only eight hours a day. The church's power was diminished and its property taken over by the government. Wages and prices were controlled. National groups and minorities were granted rights they had not had before. Education was now to be free. Women were proclaimed, in the eyes of the law, equal to men. A Red Army (red became the national color) was formed under the brilliant and skillful tactics of Trotsky and all men were to receive military training.

Soon after Lenin's seizure of power, troubles began to mount at home. To make matters worse, German troops were practically at the outskirts of Petrograd. The Ukrainians, wanting their independence, began to rebel. The cossacks and other dissatisfied military forces were threatening to start a counterrevolutionary campaign against Lenin's fledgling regime. Then troops from the Allies, the United States, France, and England entered Russia, seemingly to hold off a German invasion, but also to lend support to formidable anti-Bolshevik army units that were beginning to harass people and besiege places loyal to Lenin and his revolution. These contingents, called "Whites," were bitterly opposed to the Communists, or Reds, as they were now being called.

The Allies had a great dilemma: whether or not to intervene in Russia. To start an eastern front against Germany was now meaningless. Should they identify with the pre-Bolshevik Russians who fought on their side during the war? Were the Communists getting aid from Germany to build up their forces? Could the Communist regime in Moscow, with its determination to spread revolution, become a menace to all of Europe?

On the other hand, by now the Allies were too tired of war and had suffered too many casualties to fight more major battles in distant Russia. There was a call to bring the boys home. Besides there was a growing opposition by organized labor in the three countries for keeping "hands off Russia." There was considerable sympathy toward the new "workers' state."

Despite Allied attempts at bringing about peace between the two warring sides, munitions and supplies were sent to the Whites. Direct intervention by Allied military forces took place on a small scale. The French withdrew their forces in the Ukraine early without hardly firing a shot. The British did some minor fighting on the northern front and also landed at Baku on the Caspian Sea and in Vladivostok on the Pacific Ocean, along with troops from the United States. Soviet Russia found herself menaced and cut off from the seas and isolated from other nations.

The Whites were comprised of former officials, nobles, bourgeoisie, gentry, military men, and clergy. They hated Lenin and the new system, referring to it as the "Red Menace." All signs pointed to the possibility that a civil war was in the making.

Lenin was convinced that he had to live up to his word and make peace with Germany. The Germans knew that the

Communists were unable to fight against them at the same time they were fighting enemies on the home front. In the Treaty of Brest-Litovsk in 1918, which ended Russia's involvement in World War I, Lenin was humiliated. He was forced to give up one-third of Russia's population and one-fourth of its territory, including valuable farming and industrial areas. But, in the back of his mind, he expected the German kaiser, like the tsar, to be overthrown by the rising tide of socialism in that country as well. Then, he surmised, the two nations would cooperate in bringing down other capitalistic regimes in Europe, thus minimizing the effects of the treaty. Unfortunately for Lenin, his plan never materialized.

To complicate things even more, Lenin and his aides decided to move the Russian capital away from the Whites in Petrograd to Moscow. Once in Moscow, Lenin moved into an office and modest five-room apartment in the Kremlin, a walled-in citadel from which the tsars had ruled centuries before.

Once in the Kremlin, Lenin took on the role of supreme ruler. The war was over, but there was no peace within the country. Russia went through a grim and violent time. Anarchy, despair, and terrorism gripped the entire nation. For Lenin, it seemed that the more things changed, the more they stayed the same. Disgruntled Russians were often, in the eyes of the new government, considered enemies of the state. The Cheka, the brutal and ruthless secret police, were ordered by Lenin to step up efforts to put down all opposition. They went on a rampage arresting and murdering "counterrevolutionaries." Tens of thousands of people were sent to forced labor camps and mines.

Opposition to Lenin's eight-month-long regime burst into a savage civil war by the summer of 1918. For three years battles were fought between the White and Red armies on many fronts from Siberia to Poland. Fifteen thousand Czech soldiers and many Poles joined in the fight against the Communists as well. Countless numbers of nonbelligerents were swept into the hostilities. An untold number perished. Hundreds of towns were plundered and put to the torch.

The tragedy of the civil war, with its huge waste of human lives and tremendous destruction of property, detracted from the program hoped for by the Communist leaders. Consequently Lenin and his commissars had to resort to their own tough measures to repress a rebellion. The crisis in the country became so severe and the threat of collapse of the government so real that the Soviet government had to concentrate all its energies to maintain its power. Ideals had to be compromised for expediency.

When in March 1921 sailors of the Kronstadt naval fortress in Petrograd rebelled, Lenin called upon large battalions of the Red Army, now five million strong under Trotsky, to suppress the uprising. The number of killed and wounded on both sides was in the thousands. And eight thousand sailors were forced to flee to Finland. In spite of all the attempts of the counterrevolutionaries, the Communists managed to defend the Soviet power.

By 1921 the war had ended. The White armies were crushed. Foreign armies left Russian soil. But the price paid for victory was high. Millions of people had been killed. A prolonged drought from 1921 to 1922 caused a great famine. Perhaps as many as seven million died from hunger and epidemics in the first two and one-half years of Soviet rule. The country was in ruins. Food, relief aid, and tons of supplies from different foreign countries, organizations, and unions of workers (including the United States), were sent to war-torn Russia, along with experts from many different fields to help the Russian people get off to a new start.

One of the new starts introduced by Lenin was his New Economic Policy, known as the NEP. Lenin had tried since 1917 to set up a system of militant communism. By 1920 he was wise enough to see that the economy was crumbling and nothing seemed to be working as Marx and Engels had predicted. The production of goods and services fell drastically. Lenin suspected that some workers and managers, not devoted enough to the Communist principles, were deliberately holding back on their jobs. He charged thousands with "economic sabotage." Hundreds were jailed or shot.

The existing system, without private ownership and

limited incentives and higher salaries for skilled administrators, proved to be a failure. Lenin thought that perhaps the transition had gone too far, too fast. Besides, the idea of running a factory by committees of workers proved worthless. Then late in February 1921, Lenin, once again showing his pragmatic side, proposed a series of drastic changes to the current laws. The party agreed with him that these changes had to be made, but only until the economy could be improved. Then Russia would revert to its original Socialist management.

The new economic policy would combine Communist doctrines with various features of capitalism, a sort of compromise. Lenin had to do this to save the country from going under. Private buying and selling would be permitted. The government would be financed by taxes, instead of allowing bureaucrats simply to take supplies from the peasants and redistribute them according to need.

Almost immediately the economy picked up. Thousands of workers, prompted by an appeal by Lenin, went to the villages to help peasants organize collective farms. Industrial and farm production climbed. Electrification of the country was started. The people's morale improved because there was a steady flow of goods and foodstuffs between cities and villages. The Soviet Republic was slowly growing after the devastating civil war. Still Lenin was unwilling to put any power back into the hands of the people.

Lenin and Krupskaya in Gorki, 1922

Chapter 12

LENIN DIES

In spite of his dynamic character, his ample physical strength, and his usual attention to exercise and healthful living, Lenin did not have perfect health. He had a number of ailments he never shared with the public. Most of his life he suffered from headaches and insomnia.

From August 30, 1918, until the day he died, Lenin lived with a bullet in his neck as a result of an assassination attempt. Faina (Fanya) Kaplan, a young woman with a history of mental illness, fired three close-range shots at Lenin, declaring that he had betrayed the revolution. Ironically, he had just completed a speech to workers about the danger of counterrevolutionary activities. Kaplan was immediately arrested and executed four days later. The incident triggered a massive hunt for hundreds of other counterrevolutionaries. With Lenin's approval, many were imprisoned or shot by Cheka officials in a campaign of "Red Terror" against "White Terror."

Even Krupskaya had noted unhappily that her husband had changed during the months he had been in power. He appeared to be harder and colder than before. When she posed a question to him about the need for taking such harsh measures, she was shocked with his blunt reply: "If we don't shoot a few of the leaders opposed to us now, we may have to shoot ten thousand workers who will follow them, later on."

In many ways Lenin possessed a dual personality. He could be extremely ruthless, willing to destroy the lives of hundreds of thousands blocking his path to power, both the innocent and the guilty. On the other hand, he was obsessed with his heartfelt commitment and actions to improve human conditions and ethics based on what he deemed to be the highest ideals. Lenin was at times simultaneously materialistic and idealistic. He was an opportunist. Compromise could be a political expediency if in the end it enabled ultimate goals to be reached. But he never compromised his views of atheism. He resorted to dictatorial means in a society intended to be democratic. He was not a fiery speaker, yet he had an uncanny ability to inspire people and garner their respect and loyalty.

Had Lenin not become seriously ill after the revolution and had he not died during the early formative stages of his country's emergence as a soviet state, it is probable that many of his plans eventually would have been realized. And the history of the USSR and the world would have been appreciably altered during most of the twentieth century.

Though Lenin recuperated reasonably well, it is suspected that his injuries may have contributed to a series of health problems in the years thereafter. For his convalescence Lenin and Krupskaya went to Gorki, a lovely village about thirty miles outside Moscow. They stayed at an elegant estate formerly owned by a rich textile manufacturer. At the end of May 1922, while resting at Gorki, Lenin suffered the first of two strokes that afflicted him that year. A third, in 1923, resulted in his loss of speech.

Though Lenin was impaired by his long bouts with illness, he fought back with great courage and perseverance. On good days his mind was still sharp. With the help of Krupskaya and his sister Maria, he could walk about, but later needed a wheelchair. He even taught himself to write again, using his left hand.

Over extended periods of rest and confinement in Gorki, Lenin's direct involvement in matters of running the government was restricted. His work schedule at the Kremlin was limited. His visitors at Gorki were confined to his family and top Kremlin leaders, including Stalin and Trotsky (each had an intense dislike of the other). Being fond of children all his life, Lenin cherished the moments when children would call, or he could attend a village children's party. During his final months, Lenin enjoyed visits from his nephew Victor, the son of his younger brother, Dimitri.

Of great concern to Lenin, as he began to realize that his death was approaching, was the question of who would succeed him. Stalin, during the period of Lenin's deteriorating health, had been maneuvering to concentrate great power in his hands. Lenin, though, had great distrust of Stalin. He did not respect his intellect, deemed him unpredictable, and felt that he was too crude and rude to become the leader of the Russian people. In Lenin's eyes Stalin was too vicious a man to reroute the revolution to true socialism.

The temperature outside Lenin's Gorki residence on the night of January 21, 1924, was 30 degrees below zero. Lenin died that night in the upstairs bedroom of the big house precisely at 6:50 P.M. All the mirrors were covered at once, according to Russian tradition. Every clock in the house was stopped at 6:50 and they have remained that way ever since. Lenin was fifty-four years old.

Six days later, on Sunday, January 27, hundreds of thousands of people lined the streets of Moscow in the bitter cold to pay their last respects to Lenin during his funeral procession. Then his body lay in state while tens of thousands filed past in tribute.

And today, tens of thousands still file past his embalmed body on display in a tomb, on Red Square, just outside the Kremlin walls.

Lenin (Vladimir Ilyich Ulyanov) 1870-1924

1870 Vladimir Ilyich Ulyanov is born in Simbirsk, Russia. The Franco-Prussian War begins. Jules Verne writes *Twenty Thousand Leagues Under the Sea*. Heinrich Schliemann begins to excavate Troy.

1871 Lewis Carroll writes *Through the Looking Glass*. Charles Darwin writes *The Descent of Man*. Giuseppi Verdi composes *Aida*. The Great Fire burns in Chicago. The first modern luxury liner, the S.S. *Oceanic*, is launched.

1872 Grigori Rasputin, the Russian monk, is born. Ulysses S. Grant is reelected president of the U.S. Jules Verne writes *Around the World in Eighty Days*. James Abbott McNeil Whistler paints a portrait of his mother. The Brooklyn Bridge is opened.

1873 The first oil well in Russia is sunk at Baku. Color photographs are developed.

1874 Benjamin Disraeli becomes prime minister of Great Britain. Herbert Hoover is born. Winston Churchill is born. The first impressionist art exhibit is held in Paris. Pressure cooking is introduced as a method for canning foods.

1875 Britain buys shares in the Suez Canal. Korea becomes an independent nation. *Trial by Jury*, the first Gilbert and Sullivan operetta, is produced.

1876 Colorado becomes a state. Mark Twain writes *The Adventures of Tom Sawyer*. Alexander Graham Bell invents the telephone.

1877 Queen Victoria (Great Britain) is proclaimed Empress of India. Rutherford B. Hayes is inaugurated as the nineteenth president of the U.S. Thomas Edison invents the phonograph. Leo Tolstoy writes *Anna Karenina*.

1878 An anti-Socialist law is enacted in Germany. Gilbert and Sullivan write *Pinafore*. Electric street lighting is introduced in London.

1879 Joseph Stalin is born. Leon Trotsky is born. Pyotr Ilich Tchaikovsky's opera *Eugene Onegin* is presented in Moscow. Fyodor Dostoyevsky writes *The Brothers Karamazov*. Albert Einstein is born. Thomas Alva Edison and Joseph Swan independently devise the first practical electric lights.

1880 Disraeli resigns as British prime minister; William Gladstone succeeds him. New York streets are first lit by electricity.

1881 Tsar Alexander II is assassinated. James Garfield is inaugurated as twentieth president of the U.S. He is shot and killed in September and is succeeded by Vice-President Chester A. Arthur. Disraeli dies. Dostoyevsky dies. Pablo Picasso is born.

1882 Franklin D. Roosevelt is born. Robert Louis Stevenson writes *Treasure Island*.

1883 Karl Marx dies. The Metropolitan Opera House in New York is opened. The first skyscraper (ten stories) is built in Chicago. Buffalo Bill organizes his first Wild West Show.

1884 Grover Cleveland is elected U.S. president. Harry S. Truman is born. Mark Twain writes *Huckleberry Finn*. The first underground tube opens in London.

1885 The Congo (Africa) becomes a personal possession of the king of Belgium. Gilbert and Sullivan present *The Mikado* in London. George Eastman manufactures coated photographic paper.

1886 Lenin's father dies. Gladstone introduces a bill for home rule for Ireland. Karl Marx's *Das Kapital* is published in English. The Canadian Pacific Railway is completed.

1887 Lenin's brother Alexander is arrested in St. Petersburg in an attempt to assassinate Tsar Alexander III and is executed by hanging. Lenin enters the University of Kazan. Queen Victoria celebrates her golden jubilee. The first Sherlock Holmes story is written by A. Conan Doyle. Celluloid film is invented.

1888 Eastman perfects the Kodak box camera. John Dunlop invents the pneumatic tire.

1889 Benjamin Harrison inaugurated as twenty-third president of the U.S. Adolf Hitler is born. Charlie Chaplin is born. The Eiffel Tower is designed for the Paris World Exposition. Barnum and Bailey's Circus opens in London.

1890 The Swiss government introduces social insurance. Rubber gloves are used in surgery for the first time. The first entirely steel-framed building is built in Chicago.

1891 Lenin passes his law examination with a perfect score (and without attending classes). Wireless telegraphy is invented. Construction of the Trans-Siberian Railroad begins. There is widespread famine in Russia.

1892 Lenin begins the practice of law in Samara. Grover Cleveland is elected president of the U.S. Tchaikovsky's *Nutcracker* ballet is performed in St. Petersburg. The first automatic telephone switchboard is introduced. The first cans of pineapple appear.

1893 Lenin moves to St. Petersburg where he begins Socialist propaganda work. Hawaii is annexed to the U.S. A World Exposition is held in Chicago.

1894 Tsar Nicholas II succeeds his father Alexander III.

1895 Lenin is arrested and imprisoned in St. Petersburg. He begins writing *The Development of Capitalism in Russia*. Cuba fights Spain for its independence. The first public film is shown in Paris. Tchaikovsky's ballet *Swan Lake* is performed in St. Petersburg. William Conrad Roentgen discovers X-rays. Guglielmo Marconi invents wireless telegraphy. Auguste and Louis Lumière invent a motion-picture camera. King Gillette invents the safety razor.

1896 Tsar Nicholas II visits Paris and London. William McKinley is elected twenty-fifth president of the U.S. Nobel prizes are established.

1897 Lenin is exiled to Siberia. Leon Trotsky forms South Russian Workers' Union. Queen Victoria celebrates her diamond jubilee.

1898 Lenin marries Nadezhda Krupskaya. The first "congress" of Socialists held in Minsk; Social Democratic party founded. Trotsky arrested. The U.S. declares war on Spain over Cuba. Pierre and Marie Curie discover radium. Ferdinand Zeppelin invents his airship. The Paris Metro is opened. U.S. annexes Hawaii.

1899 The first peace conference is held at The Hague. The first magnetic recording of sound is made. The Philippines demand independence from the U.S.

1900 Lenin completes his exile in Siberia, returns to European Russia and later moves to Switzerland; founds *Iskra* (The Spark), a revolutionary journal, intended for circulation in Russia. Boxer uprisings take place in China against the Europeans. Hawaii becomes a territory of the U.S. The Commonwealth of Australia is created. A World Exposition opens in Paris.

1901 Queen Victoria dies and is succeeded by Edward VII. President McKinley is assassinated and is succeeded by Theodore Roosevelt. A treaty is signed for the building of the Panama Canal under U.S. supervision. Walt Disney is born. Ragtime jazz develops in the U.S. Marconi transmits transatlantic radio messages.

1902 Leon Trotsky escapes from a Siberian prison and settles in London. *What Is To Be Done?* is published. The U.S. acquires control over the Panama Canal. Beatrix Potter writes *Peter Rabbit*. J.M. Bacon becomes the first man to cross the English Channel in a balloon.

1903 Lenin attends his first meeting of the Congress of the Social Democratic party in Brussels (moved to London). Bitter quarreling erupts between the Lenin and the Plekhanov factions. The party divides into the Bolsheviks and the Mensheviks. Lenin and Trotsky lead the Bolsheviks. Anti-Jewish pogroms take place in Russia. The Wright brothers fly a powered airplane successfully. The first motor taxis appear in London.

1904 The Russo-Japanese War breaks out. Lenin writes a document against the Mensheviks: *One Step Forward, Two Steps Backward*. The first railroad tunnel is built under the Hudson River between New York and New Jersey. A subway is built in New York. In New York, a woman is arrested for smoking a cigarette in public. Theodore Roosevelt wins the U.S. presidential election.

1905 On Bloody Sunday a demonstration is brutally crushed by the police in St. Petersburg. The first workers' soviet is formed. There is a general strike in Russia. The tsar promises reforms. Albert Einstein formulates the Theory of Relativity. The first neon sign appears. The first motorbuses run in London.

1906 Lenin attends the unification congress in Stockholm, Sweden. Reform laws are passed in Russia. The term "allergy" is first used in medicine. The Simplon Tunnel between Italy and Switzerland is opened. San Francisco suffers an earthquake that kills 700 people.

1907 Lenin attends Congress of the United party in London, meets Stalin. Rasputin gains influence at the court of Tsar Nicholas II. A process for color photography is developed.

1908 William Howard Taft is elected president of the U.S. Kenneth Grahame writes *Wind in the Willows*. The first steel and glass building is erected in Berlin. Fountain pens become popular.

1909 Sigmund Freud lectures in the U.S. on psychoanalysis. Louis Bleriot crosses the English Channel in an airplane. U.S. explorer Robert Peary reaches the North Pole.

1910 Lenin attends the meeting of the Socialist International held in Copenhagen; he is bitterly criticized for bringing disunity to the movement. King Edward VII of England dies and is succeeded by George V. The first deep-sea research expedition is undertaken.

1911 Roald Amundsen reaches the South Pole. Charles Kettering develops the first practical electric self-starter for automobiles.

1912 Woodrow Wilson wins the U.S. presidential election. The S.S. *Titanic* sinks on her maiden voyage and 1,500 people are drowned. The first parachute jump is successful.

1913 Demonstrations are held in London for women's suffrage. Henry Ford pioneers assemblyline techniques in his automobile factory. The Panama Canal is opened for shipping. Grand Central terminal opens in New York.

1914 Archduke Francis Ferdinand, heir to the Austrian throne, is assassinated; World War I begins. Lenin and his wife settle in Berne, Switzerland. Russia suffers great losses on the battlefield. Charlie Chaplin makes several films. The name of St. Petersburg is changed to Petrograd.

1915 Henry Ford develops a farm tractor. Alexander Graham Bell makes a transatlantic phone call. Motorized taxis appear.

1916 Wilson is reelected president of the U.S. The Russian monk Rasputin dies. Blood for transfusions is refrigerated. Jazz sweeps the U.S.

1917 There is a revolution in Russia; the tsar abdicates. The Bolsheviks overthrow the provisional government. Lenin is appointed chief commissar. A German-Russian armistice is signed. The Trans-Siberian Railroad is completed.

1918 The Russian assembly in Petrograd is dissolved by the Bolsheviks. The Soviet government is transferred to Moscow. A new Soviet constitution is written. Wilson propounds his Fourteen Points for Peace. An armistice is signed between the U.S. and Germany. An attempt is made on Lenin's life in Moscow. Tsar Nicholas II and his family are executed. Harlow Shapley, an American astronomer, discovers the true dimensions of the Milky Way. Regular airmail service is established between New York and Washington.

1919 The Bolsheviks overcome the White Russians. Observations of the total eclipse of the sun confirm Einstein's theory of relativity. The first experiments with short-wave radio are carried out.

1920 Warren G. Harding is elected president of the U.S. The surgeon Harvey Cushing develops new techniques in brain surgery. Mohandas Gandhi emerges as the leader in India's struggle for independence. Adolf Hitler announces his 25-point program at Munich.

1921 Lenin proposes sweeping new economic policies for the USSR. A tuberculosis vaccine is developed. Albert Einstein receives the Nobel prize. The Ku Klux Klan becomes violent throughout the U.S.

1922 Lenin suffers a stroke. Gandhi is sentenced to six years in prison for civil disobedience. Joseph Stalin becomes secretary-general of the Communist party.

1923 Lenin suffers a second stroke. Russia officially becomes the Union of Soviet Socialist Republics.

1924 Lenin dies. Britain recognizes the USSR. Calvin Coolidge wins the U.S. presidential election. Insecticides are used for the first time. Petrograd is renamed Leningrad.

INDEX- *Page numbers in boldface type indicate illustrations.*

129

ABOUT THE AUTHOR

Abraham Resnick, a native New Jerseyan, is a noted author and educator specializing in elementary and secondary social studies education. Dr. Resnick has had an outstanding career as a professor, writer, supervisor, consultant, and professional leader in the social sciences. His writings include text and trade books for children, teachers' editions of school materials, published resource units, map transparencies, and professional books and articles. Dr. Resnick has written two books in Childrens Press's Enchantment of the World series; *Russia: A History to 1917* and *The Union of Soviet Socialist Republics.*

He is presently serving as Professor of Education at Jersey City State College (New Jersey) and for many years was the Director of the Instructional Materials Center, Rutgers Graduate School of Education. In 1975 he was the recipient of that school's Alumni Award for Distinguished Service to Education.

Much of the research for this book was carried out in the Soviet Union during the spring of 1986. As an officially invited guest of the Soviet Union, Dr. Resnick visited museums, libraries, institutes, homes, offices, and historic sites relating to the life of Vladimir Ilyich Ulyanov—Lenin. He also had the opportunity of conferring with a number of experts specializing in various phases of Lenin's life.

Dr. Resnick's itinerary took him to Ulyanovsk (Simbirsk) on the Volga River, where Lenin spent his early years; to Leningrad (St. Petersburg and later Petrograd); to Moscow; to the village of Shushenskoye, deep in Siberia, the place of Lenin's exile; and also to Gorki, the site of Lenin's death in 1924.

When he isn't writing or teaching, Abe Resnick enjoys watching professional sporting events, playing tennis, long distance walking, bike riding, and travel to remote regions of the world.